positive thinking, positive living

positive thinking, **positive living**

Dr David Fong

Published 2014 by Geddes & Grosset,
an imprint of The Gresham Publishing Company Ltd.,
Academy Park, Building 4000, Gower Street, Glasgow, G51 1PR

First published by Geddes & Grosset in 2005 as
Not Another Self-Help Book. This edition published 2014.

Text by Dr David Fong

Cartoons by Mark Mechan

ISBN 978 1 84205 801 5

Printed and bound in the EU

Dr David Fong has written several articles for *My Weekly* magazine and also contributed a chapter to the book *Guide to Wellbeing*, published by Geddes & Grosset. He is a Chartered Doctor of Clinical Psychology and has appeared as an expert witness for the British Psychological Society. Dr Fong has also worked as an independent expert witness in childcare hearings. Perhaps more interestingly, he has also played in several disastrous rock bands and completely failed to sell his first novel. He wrote this book whilst working as an English teacher in Italy. He is short for his age.

This book is dedicated to my parents and family, who I love very much, and who I refuse to blame for anything except buying me a football for my ninth birthday instead of the motorised Batmobile I wanted. It is also dedicated to the various friendly bears, aliens and kats (sic) that have enhanced my life.

Contents

Contents

Contents

Introduction

Is your life story going to be a gripping bestseller or a resignation letter?

When I was a little boy, my comic books were full of advertisements at the back that promised me "A perfect body in 10 days or your money back!" Needless to say, I am still waiting, both for my perfect body and for my money back. Nowadays, as well as ordering physical perfection from the back pages of a magazine, you can find bookshop shelves creaking with titles that offer you emotional and spiritual completion at the drop of a hat. You can "Feel The Fear And Do It Anyway", drink "Chicken Soup For The Soul" and take a hundred other different remedies that are on offer for those who like neither soup nor fear. Needless to say, people don't seem to be getting any happier.

So why is this book any different from the others?

Firstly, this book doesn't offer you Nirvana in a week. The techniques and ideas outlined in it work, but their success depends on you. The main theme of this book is that you are responsible for your life and all that happens in it: the successes, the failures, the triumphs and the disasters. It is neither a psychology manual nor a religious textbook. I don't make any claims to it being a guide to spiritual wellbeing. Instead, this book will act as a support for you, but it will assume that you will do all the hard work. Hopefully, some of your ideas about the world and about yourself will be shaken up a little along the way.

Secondly, this book assumes that you live in the real world. If you live in a reality where everyone is blissfully happy and the idea of having a problem with something is considered quaint, then this little tome is not for you. Likewise, if you never have to worry about what the kids are going to want for their dinner; why your girlfriend isn't talking to you any more or why you are crying all the time, then this isn't the volume for you. But . . . if you find that time is flying and you're getting older but not wiser; if those unfinished projects are still unfinished; if the relationship that was going to be different from the last one ended in tears that were just as painful, then welcome! You're in the right place.

Thirdly, the ideas and exercises in this book are designed to be practical, fun and different, but with a serious point attached to them. That doesn't mean that this is a complicated academic textbook. The only qualifications that you need to use this book are:

- A desire to change something in your life and a willingness to try something new
- A sense of humour
- The belief that life is often not the way that you would want it to be

If any or all of these apply to you, then I hope you stick around and see what awaits you in the pages to come. If this isn't for you, then, that's fine – I won't be bitter. If you're not sure, why not flick through the pages at random, stop at any one that takes your fancy and see what it has to say to you? Interesting things can happen when we take even the smallest of chances.

Chapter One

New Rules

In which we discover the true costs of three TVs, microwave ovens and stress

Hands up everyone who is perfectly happy!

Unless you've been taking your holidays on Mars for the last few years, you will have noticed that the society that we are all a part of has been changing very rapidly. Some of these changes have been obvious and some less so, but they all have something in common – they have altered and shaped our lifestyles in some fundamental ways.

For example:

- People no longer believe strongly in a job for life or that the state will look after them once they have finished working. As a result, although

In which we discover the true costs of three TVs, microwave ovens and stress

people have more job flexibility, they are far more focussed on money as their only criteria for success.

- Similarly, marriage is no longer seen as "for life" – all newly-weds hope that it will be, but this is no longer the absolute that it once was. Also, not being married or in a relationship no longer carries the stigma it used to.
- The internet and satellite television have created a vast information superhighway where we are told what to buy, how to dress and sometimes, what to think; advertising is everywhere.
- Organised religion does not carry the moral authority it held in the past. In general, church attendances are falling and there doesn't seem to be anything to fill the gap.

All these fundamental changes mean that we have to face a vast number of choices with very little guidance on what the right ones are, and we have to do it everyday. Sometimes, it is easy to feel that we are making it up as we go along, a feeling that rightly scares the pants off us – generally, human beings don't like to think that they don't know what they're doing. But if we polled

*In which we discover the true costs of three TVs,
microwave ovens and stress*

a hundred people and asked them (honestly)
about their state of mind at any one time, we'd
probably get a response such as this:

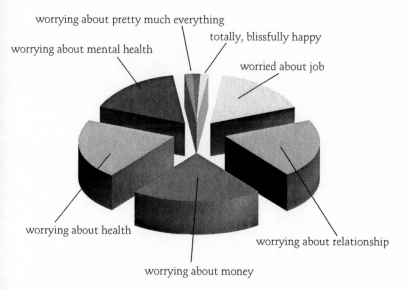

In other words, on any given day, the vast
majority of us are worried about something to a
greater or lesser degree. It seems fair to say that
living in the modern world presents us with a

*In which we discover the true costs of three TVs,
microwave ovens and stress*

strange equation: **more lifestyle choices +
more information doesn't always equal
more happiness**.

The result is what I call New Rule Number
One of Modern Life:

**Having problems is more normal than not
having problems!**

Don't panic

This concept is not meant to scare anybody; it is
meant to reassure you. Living in today's world
can be tough and sometimes it can feel as though
there are almost too many things to cope with. It
can feel as if worrying is as natural as breathing.

This is normal

We wake up to be confronted by the early morning news. Up-to-the-minute programmes relay
scenes of misery, heartbreak and political treach-
ery into our living rooms. We climb into our
overpriced cars for the drive to work. The roads
are busier and more congested than ever before

*In which we discover the true costs of three TVs,
microwave ovens and stress*

and to make things really interesting, there is the
ever-present spectre of one of our more charming American imports – road rage. We arrive at
work and the boss is shouting at everyone within earshot because her boss has just shouted at
her. Stale sandwiches for lunch. We get home
to find that our partner isn't speaking to us because we forgot their birthday. Stale sandwiches
for tea. We turn on the TV to try and relax and
four different companies are all trying to sell us
cars that would enhance our sex appeal, impress
our work colleagues and financially cripple us,
all in one shrewd move. Then the news comes
on again and we decide to stagger to bed, not
entirely convinced that in a few days' time we
will be able to remember anything other than
the slightest detail of our day.

This is normal

As a result, we decide that there's nothing we can
do to change the world or our place in it; that any
relationship is better than no relationship, so long
as we don't have to face it all alone. We come to
the conclusion that it's worth racking up huge

*In which we discover the true costs of three TVs,
microwave ovens and stress*

amounts of debt to buy things that we don't really want or need, partly because everyone else is doing it and partly because we are told every day that this is the key to happiness. We decide that continuing to do a job that we don't really like is better than taking the risk of ending up with no job at all. Then when we go to bed at night, we convince ourselves that things will be OK as long as we don't make any waves.

This is normal

If any, or all of that sounds in the least familiar, please draw comfort from the fact that you are not alone. My New Rule Number Two of Modern Living is:

Just because something is normal doesn't mean you have to accept it

Learning how to juggle

There is some great news to be had amidst these difficult choices, frantic lifestyles and advertisements on television, because one of the choices that we can make, more easily than most, is the

In which we discover the true costs of three TVs, microwave ovens and stress

decision to change things. There are stories about people changing their lives every day on the television – for example, giving up a successful job in the City to go and work as a sheepherder in Australia. But it is important to note that significant change doesn't have to be outwardly dramatic. People leave unhappy relationships and unhappy marriages and strive to find something better for themselves, not because of some moral failing or lack of determination on their part, but because they have made a choice and are ready to face the consequences. A situation may be normal, usual, or routine – but that doesn't mean that it has to stay that way forever.

People who make successful life-changing decisions tend to:

• *Plan the details carefully*

Life changing decisions – whether that's going to live in another country, or to change the way we think – that are made on the spur of the moment can backfire and although such events often teach us a lot, anticipating such outcomes before they happen can be very helpful.

*In which we discover the true costs of three TVs,
microwave ovens and stress*

• *Talk it over*

Friends and family can be fantastic sounding boards when we have a decision to make. Even if they tell us that we are crazy and we should go back to our day jobs, such contrary opinions can really help us to decide where we stand.

• *Use their skills*

Making big decisions takes effort, patience, and organisation. It also takes honesty (to decide to make the decision in the first place) and it takes courage to stick with the decision once it has been made. People often discover that they have skills and abilities that they never knew they had – or had forgotten they possessed – and it can be a real character boost to realise that you can confront something head on.

• *Use fear positively*

Fear is inevitable when we make decisions that deeply affect our lives. Imagine a teacher who decides she has had enough of teaching and wants to become a florist. Imagine how scared she would be and the thoughts that would run through her head – *what if I don't make any money? What if the business fails?* Now imagine that, even in the face of these fears, she continues with her plan. She uses her fear to check if she is still doing the right thing, rather than letting it paralyse her. Obstacles become challenges. Now, imagine how good she'll feel when she succeeds!

• *Stay focussed and rely on themselves*
It is easier to have focus, enthusiasm and spirit at the beginning of a project than it is half way through. People who follow through on their decisions keep their focus and come to rely on it, even through the difficult times, because they believe that it will be worth it in the end.

It seems that we can look at life in one of two ways. We can view ourselves as struggling under the burden of too many things to do and not enough time to do them in, back ourselves into impossible corners and spend time worrying about where our lives are going. Or we can think of the image on one of the Tarot cards (a set of cards used for fortune-telling and personal discovery) that shows a young man cheerfully juggling a number of brightly coloured spheres and dancing. It is equally valid to view life in

In which we discover the true costs of three TVs,
microwave ovens and stress

this way – a delicate juggling act that needs our skills, attention and the ability to drop something old and pick up something new. People can come to view obstacles as challenges that will enable them to learn new skills, rather than insurmountable problems. But, just like juggling, this needs practise. We also have to know what to change first – hopefully, you wouldn't start to learn how to juggle using kitchen knives!

So where do I start?

We know that every day, we are confronted by a whole host of choices, and that there are more opportunities than ever before to take advantage of them. We also know that successful people make decisions that they have carefully planned out first. Part of the planning involves knowing exactly what it is that you want to change before you change it. It is a bit like looking at a jigsaw puzzle and working out which bits fit and which don't. For example, on the top left of the figure below, we can imagine this jigsaw piece represents our relationships with other people – partners, friends, work colleagues, and so on.

In which we discover the true costs of three TVs, microwave ovens and stress

What part of this jigsaw piece do we want to change? Maybe we feel we are spending too much time with our work colleagues and not enough time with our partner. So, in the area of relationships we know that a few adjustments need to be made and knowing where to start means the changes are more likely to be effective – we're not just changing things for change's sake.

Perhaps the top right figure is our work life. Is this piece bigger than all the other pieces? Are

*In which we discover the true costs of three TVs,
microwave ovens and stress*

we happy about that? How will we adjust this? Sometimes, when work takes over our lives, we either let it, or try and make all the other pieces bigger, which can result in us burning the candle at both ends. Perhaps we need to find another way to make this important piece of our lifestyle jigsaw fit more comfortably with the rest.

We could imagine that the bottom left hand piece is our free time spent out of work. Is this a healthy colour or is it looking a bit drab? Does it look rather sad and small next to the work piece? And what about the bottom right piece – our hopes, dreams, ambitions and plans for the future? When did we last really spent time looking at this piece, thinking about how it has changed over the years and whether it still has a place for us in our lifestyle jigsaw? This, too, may need a bit of careful attention.

Draw your own lifestyle jigsaw

Try drawing either your own jigsaw, with the relevant colours for your lifestyle, or sketch a picture of yourself juggling, or a set of playing cards with the different areas of your life on each one. It can be easy to forget all the different things in

*In which we discover the true costs of three TVs,
microwave ovens and stress*

our lives, and quite surprising to see where all our time goes. Before changing anything, you need to know what it is you're trying to change – this is all part of the preparation you need to make. Keep your drawing with you and look at it again in a few months. How has it changed? Is it closer to how you wanted it to look or even further away? What changes were successful and which ones were not? Once we know what the different areas of our lives look like and what they involve, it is easier to think about making changes. However, that is often where the problems start.

Why don't we make changes?

Sometimes we don't make the changes that we want to because of unforeseen circumstances. If we suffer a bereavement, a sudden loss of income, or something happens that we couldn't foresee, it is easy for this to throw us off our stride and interfere with even the most careful preparations. Then we face an altogether different challenge – that of coming to terms with what has happened. It is at times like these that we can be reminded of human beings' remarkable ability to adapt to adversity.

*In which we discover the true costs of three TVs,
microwave ovens and stress*

There is an answer to the question above, which may surprise those of you who consider yourselves intelligent, rational, sensible broad-minded people (which most of us do). For the vast majority of cases, the thing that really stands in our way when we are trying to make decisions is . . . ourselves.

*In which we discover the true costs of three TVs,
microwave ovens and stress*

Sound familiar?

In which we discover the true costs of three TVs, microwave ovens and stress

Give yourself a slap on the wrist for every time you've let one of these thoughts influence whether you change something or not. It is easy, however, to see how these thoughts can really affect our drive and motivation to do something. This is an issue that we will look at later in the book – we'll also investigate the steps we can take to remedy these situations. For now, it is enough to realise how self-defeating we can all be – imagine if we had these negative thoughts all the time. How much confidence would we have in ourselves? Would we have any confidence in our ability to change anything, or would we passively accept our lot?

The next question that arises is – where do these thoughts come from?

And for that – it's on to chapter two.

STRESS

One of the things that can seriously affect our ability to make decisions is stress. Stress is a modern day phenomenon that has entered our lexicon without us even being aware of it. "I'm so stressed out", "I can't cope with all this stress", even "he's taking a few days off work with stress" have become common laments. Stress can be seen as a classic symptom of suffering a situation that will not change and feeling unable to do anything about it.

And it is something that affects us all. The statistics are staggering. Some estimates put the cost to the economy of stress at some £5 billion a year, an estimated 250,000 workers per day take time off because off stress and the problem is not going away. If anything, it is getting worse.

Some stress can be helpful. If we are completely apathetic about a task or demand, it is unlikely we will do our best. Someone who is completely relaxed will probably not perform as well as someone who is moderately anxious before an exam, all things being equal. *Negative* Stress is often defined as the demands on a person exceeding their perceived ability to cope. The psychological and physical impact on us can be tremendously wide-ranging, involving everything from relatively minor problems, such as short-temper and sleepless nights, to more serious problems such as reduced immune deficiency functioning, elevated blood pressure, depression, relationship problems and even, heart attacks. Make no mistake – stress can kill.

At times like these, it is vital to be honest with ourselves and assess the situation realistically. If there is a genuine end in sight to the stress, then it is possible to endure it, knowing that something will change in the near future. But if it is clear that the problem is not going to go away, then you must take steps to help yourself. Feeling embarrassed that "you are not coping" can be the biggest hurdle to changing the situation.

If you feel that stress is having a real impact on your life, it is important to do something about it. Consult your GP and collaborate with work colleagues to find solutions. If you find yourself thinking "I'm too busy to go the doctors with something as silly as stress", then answer this simple question – which is more important, your physical and mental wellbeing or your job? Don't wait until it's too late – act now.

Chapter Two

Why Do We Make Things Difficult For Ourselves?

In which we discover who our worst enemy is

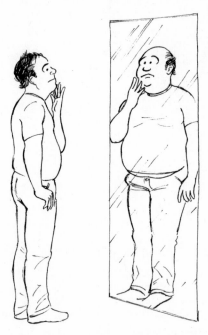

In which we discover who our worst enemy is

The Negative Command Centre

In the last chapter, we saw that life could be a double-edged sword. Firstly, there is the sharp reality that life can be filled with many difficult choices that we sometimes feel overwhelmed by. But on the flip side, there's the thrill of knowing that we have more opportunity than ever before to change things. What a fantastic opportunity! We should be jumping for joy!.

But as we discovered in the previous chapter, one of the main obstacles to changing things is ourselves. Sometimes, we struggle to make decisions because of listening to something I could call (having watched too much Star Trek as a child) the Negative Command Centre. This is the part of our brain that tries ever so hard to be helpful in times of difficulty but inevitably comes up with thoughts such as:

In which we discover who our worst enemy is

- I'm not the kind of person who makes waves
- What if it all goes wrong?
- I couldn't possibly just give up my job
- But if I leave her I'll be alone forever

You know the kind of thing. We like to think of these thoughts as the Voice of Reason, but this is actually a misnomer. The Voice of Reason tells us it is probably not a good idea to jump out of a moving vehicle at 60 miles an hour, whilst simultaneously wrestling an alligator. That's fair enough. But it's easy to confuse this voice with what we hear from the Negative Command Centre, which, as we will see, is something altogether different.

The Voice of Reason versus the Negative Command Centre

Let's quickly compare the two so that we know what we're talking about.

In which we discover who our worst enemy is

The Voice of Reason says:

In which we discover who our worst enemy is

The Voice of Reason applies very simple logic. If something is harmful to us, the Voice Of Reason will probably make itself heard at some point and instruct us to avoid it. It bases its decisions on simple, evidence-based information. We don't walk blindly into traffic because we have strong evidence that we will be hit by something. We don't drink bleach because we have learnt, and have evidence to support the idea, that it will make us very ill. We don't tend to argue with man eating tigers because our experience and all the evidence suggests that if we do, it is more than likely that we will end up as a 'McTiger Happy Meal'. We have a lot of evidence to support the claims of the Voice of Reason, which is why, as a rule, we don't argue with tigers or gargle with bleach.

In which we discover who our worst enemy is

But now compare this with the Negative Command Centre's advice:

The difference between these two voices is that the former is based on valid, reliable evidence, whereas the second is based on guesswork, supposition and often fear. The human brain is often very good at guesswork and anticipating things; for example, when we are driving our cars we are very good at guessing what might be around the next bend. But at other times, we are simply terrible at it and we follow awful advice – our own – on the basis of little or no evidence. What's worse, is that we often do nothing at all on the basis that something absolutely horrible will happen to us from which there will be no recovery if we even think of making changes.

Where do negative thoughts come from?

Let's compare the origin of the Voice of Reason and the Negative Command Centre.

The Voice of Reason is an example of how good parents can be at teaching their children about the world around them. Parents give simple commands to their children: "Don't put your hands in the fire, you'll get hurt!", "Don't stare into the sun, it'll damage your eyes!" These commands are

In which we discover who our worst enemy is

based on valid experience, valid information and valid evidence, and, as such, are difficult to argue with. As children, we carry these instructions around with us and find that they are useful and sometimes vital to our survival. As we grow older, we develop similar laws about the world around us that are generally pretty accurate: if we don't go to work, we will be fired; if we don't study, we won't do particularly well in exams, and so on.

The Negative Command Centre is a bit different. Thoughts based on this system come from a variety of sources, whereas messages from the Voice Of Reason are generally true for nearly everybody. Presumably Richard Branson doesn't get into trouble if he rolls in late for work and there are people who never appear to study and still pass their exams. The critical difference with messages from the Negative Command Centre is that we act as if they are true without stopping to check if they really are. For example, a person may say to themselves: "There's no point in me asking this person to go to the cinema with me, she'll only say no." They may say this on the basis of being rejected by a couple of other prospective partners in the past, but just because two

In which we discover who our worst enemy is

girls say one thing, doesn't mean that they will all say the same thing. Our poor Romeo acts as if this is fact, and so passes up an opportunity to start a new relationship.

Let's consider some of the other sources via which we gather instructions for our Negative Command Centre.

Parents

As every parent will testify, parenting is without question the hardest job on the face of the Earth – and children don't come with instruction manuals. It is a job that you learn as you go along and, as with every such venture, mistakes are inevitable. As adults, we can often clearly remember the times when our parents shouted at us, what they said, and the impact it has had on us.

It is extremely hard for any parent to strike a balance between overprotecting their children (so that the real world turns out to be a scary place for them once they venture out into it) and not protecting them enough (so that a child learns that the only person they can rely on is him or herself). Without meaning to, parents often give

In which we discover who our worst enemy is

their children a number of commands that they then come to believe are absolutely true, and these thoughts stick around well into adulthood. These might be relatively innocuous – "girls don't play football" – or significantly more powerful – "oh, you're so stupid! What did you do that for?" So, thoughts coming from our Negative Command Centre can be based on how we made sense of what our parents did and said.

Our environment

Prenatal: Even before a child is born, there are a myriad different influences at work. If a mother is stressed, angry, using drugs or, perhaps, depressed, there can be effects on the baby which can manifest many years later. Genetic influences play a part on development too. For example, psychologists have known for many years that a child is more likely to develop schizophrenia if both parents suffer from the illness.

Postnatal: As soon as children are born, they begin to interact with their external environment and all the things in it. As they get older, they

In which we discover who our worst enemy is

learn to interpret and make sense of all the information they receive, using some and filtering out the rest. Part of growing up is learning to make predictions about the world and this skill is vital. Imagine what life would be like if every time we met someone, we had absolutely no way of knowing how to act, no way of predicting how they would behave towards us and no way of interpreting their behaviour. But although this is a vital psychological system, it is by no means perfect.

For children, learning everything for the first time, making predictions and interpretations is extremely hard.

When a teacher shouts at them, children don't think: "Well, Mr Smith had a row with his wife last night. And I know he's having trouble with the mortgage. I mustn't take it personally."

They think in very black and white ways, "I am a bad person" or "it was my fault". These interactions with the outside world, combined with our internal interpretations of what goes on, shape how we view ourselves.

We grow up trying to make sense of all that happens and sometimes we get it wrong. And then to make it worse, we act as if it were right.

In which we discover who our worst enemy is

Problems with fortune-telling

The practice of making predictions based on our Negative Command Centre is very inexact and accuracy decreases the further into the future we try to look. For example, the woman who says "what's the point of getting involved with anyone, I know I'm always going to be alone" acts on the basis of a prediction of how her life is going to be in 40 or 50 years' time.

But our Negative Command Centre has difficulty with events in the near future, too. We are simply unable to know everything there is to know and so our brain "fills in" for us. We don't know for an absolute fact that that nice man we met at the bus stop isn't going to start hurling insults at us, or flinging his shopping into the middle of the road. We predict that he won't do any of these things, on the basis that people in general don't behave in such a way, and we would be profoundly disturbed if he did.

But our predictions about ourselves are skewed by all the influences we looked at earlier, and by many more. It is often easier to make guesses about why a stranger is behaving in a certain way

In which we discover who our worst enemy is

than to come up with reasons for our own behaviour; although, we often make a mess of both
interpretations. In the same way, we often find it
easier to give wonderful advice to our friends and
family, but find it impossible to apply the same
wisdom to our own lives.

So there are a number of problems that accompany our Negative Command Centre and the
biggest ones are these:

- The evidence that the Negative Command
  Centre uses is incomplete
- We treat thoughts coming from the Negative Command Centre as though they were
  facts
- Sometimes we have no idea where certain
  thoughts of ours come from

How do you know?

How many times have we heard ourselves saying to people the dreaded phrase "I just know?"
For example: How do you know that this relationship is going to turn out like the last? – *I just
know*. How do you know that there's no point in

In which we discover who our worst enemy is

trying for that new job? – *I just know.* How do you know she doesn't like you? – *I just know.*

We often accept this answer from both ourselves and other people because we never ask the follow up questions: What is your evidence for this? When did you get your degree in fortune-telling or mind-reading? And if you absolutely know what is going to go wrong when you try "x", why not do something about it?"

Now let's take a look in a bit more detail how our interpretations on life can lead us astray. The events on the left hand side of the chart are not uncommon and, sadly, neither are the interpretations.

In which we discover who our worst enemy is

Event	Interpretation
Birth of sibling (age four)	My parents like her better than me
Early rejection by peer group (age eight)	People don't like me
Academic criticism (age 11)	I'm stupid
Puberty (begins age 13)	I'm clumsy and awkward
Confrontation with parents (begins aged 14)	No one understands me
Early sexual or romantic experiences (age 16)	Men aren't to be trusted
First job (age 17)	I've no time to do anything I want to do
Break up of relationships (age 19)	Life can be cruel
First bereavement (age 23)	What's the point of trying anything new if nothing lasts?

In which we discover who our worst enemy is

Now, this is a very simplified table of events and life certainly isn't as clear cut as this diagram would suggest. But, as we have seen, it is common for people to believe that such statements are absolutely true. Imagine how life would be if we thought all the thoughts above had the quality of fact – the unknown would be seen as something terrifying and unbearable and we might adopt the attitude that it's better to cling onto whatever we have, than take a risk that we could change things for the better.

Coping, or following bad advice?

As a result of interpretations like these, we often adopt what psychologists call coping mechanisms. These are often ways of rationalising why we follow the advice of our Negative Command Centre, and are often formed in parallel with these thoughts. If our Negative Command Centre tells us that we are not very interesting people, perhaps we avoid parties and social gatherings as a coping mechanism because we don't want people to think that we are boring. If we treat this thought as a fact – I am boring – then when we ask ourselves how we know this, the answer will be: I just know.

In which we discover who our worst enemy is

It is easy to see how this influences our behaviour: we stay at home more frequently and decline invitations to go out. This becomes our coping strategy for being boring. Now, if we imagine how we might feel as a consequence of all this, it becomes easy to see how a vicious cycle develops.

I AM SAD

I AM BORING

I WILL STAY IN TONIGHT

In which we discover who our worst enemy is

How thoughts, feelings and actions connect

A negative feedback loop or the 'sour bagel'. Brace yourself for chapter 4, page 92 and the 'happy doughnut'

These directives from the Negative Command Centre can, therefore, be far more powerful than just influencing what we think – they can shape our lives in very fundamental ways. Things can become even more complex if we combine these directives with coping strategies that we learnt when we were younger but which are now

In which we discover who our worst enemy is

actively unhelpful. For example, the child who reacts to frustration by having a tantrum may grow up thinking that anger is the only way to solve problems.

Back to the beginning . . .

At the beginning of this chapter, I asked: why do we make things difficult for ourselves? To summarise:

- All too often we follow the advice of what I have called the Negative Command Centre. This system of thinking tries its best to give us good advice, but we tend to proceed on the basis that what it is giving us is hard fact. Actually, what it gives us are ideas from our parents, our society and interpretations of our own experience that are often incorrect.
- Thoughts don't exist in isolation but are linked to what we feel and what we do. This means that if we follow the Negative Command Centre's advice it can have powerful effects on every part of our life.
- We often learn coping strategies when we are

In which we discover who our worst enemy is

younger and, like a computer using an old system, we forget to update them. For example, teenagers who start smoking as a way of identifying themselves as cool or different from their peers (a not uncommon reason to start) find themselves at 30 still smoking and being seen not as cool and living on the edge, but as something of an eccentric.

In the next chapter, we will look in a little more detail at what happens when we make things difficult for ourselves, as well as thinking about what we can do about it.

ADDICTIONS

Addictions can be seen as a way of attempting to cope with life. Nobody starts out wanting to become an addict, whether it be to tobacco, alcohol or cocaine – the desire when indulging in any of these is to be better, happier or at the very least, to feel a bit different from normal. But whilst the majority of people don't become addicts, for some, the attempt to create a 'solution' can become a terrible problem.

Addictions can be seen as a coping mechanism that may have been useful in some way at some time. For the teenager, smoking may be a way of establishing that they are cool or somehow a bit dangerous; alcohol may be a way for someone to deaden unbearable feelings, or to help them relax socially, whilst cocaine may be a way of experimenting. The problem occurs when the reason for the use of the coping mechanism ends, but the behaviour continues. If we don't know why we are doing something, it can be very hard to stop.

Addictions to drugs (with alcohol and tobacco being by far the most damaging, regardless of what the newspapers might tell us) are often defined in terms of the cost to the user and to society. Problem drug use often involves:

- Consistent failure to fulfil responsibilities, for example, in work and parenting.
- The user getting into potentially dangerous situations.
- A threat to health and wellbeing.
- Difficulties with the law or authorities (for example, the mother who is told if she doesn't stop using amphetamines, her children will be placed in care)
- Failure to stop taking substances, despite social/interpersonal problems

It is important that we are honest with ourselves in connection with our drug use. Ask: "what is this costing me?" For those who are drinking too much, it may be the respect and trust of their families; for smokers, it is the damage to their health. No one is hurt more than us when we delude ourselves that we are just having a good time.

Chapter Three

Blame

In which a friendly alien asks us an important question

Which rules do you live by?

In the last chapter, we saw that even though life is tough enough without creating obstacles, the person whom we always fall back on for advice – ourselves – can also be the source of some of our biggest cognitive gaffes. Sometimes, we follow what appears to be helpful advice but which all too often leads us down dark alleys, following rules that are not based on hard evidence. Before we take a closer look at two of these problems, let's think about which rules you are living by.

Dr Dave's SuperFast personality quiz

Chose the answer (a) or (b) that best fits your responses to the following questions (if neither

In which a friendly alien asks us an important question

fits perfectly, pick the one that is closest to how you'd react).

A relationship has just ended. Do you think:

(a) They've ruined my life! I'll never forgive them.
(b) Why wasn't I a better girl/boyfriend? I should've tried harder.

After a row with a friend, you:

(a) Wait for them to call – it was all their fault it happened.
(b) Phone them immediately and apologise regardless of what happened.

Your bank details are at their lowest ever ebb. Do you:

(a) Have a splurge to feel better – those credit card companies are all frauds.
(b) Eat bread and cheese for a month and hate yourself for being so stupid.

You stub your toe on the kitchen table. You think:

(a) Stupid, idiotic table!
(b) Why did I put that there?

In which a friendly alien asks us an important question

Your boss criticises your work. Before he has time to explain, you:

(a) Launch a stinging attack on his management techniques – he can't talk to you like that!
(b) Promise to redouble your work efforts immediately.

If you answered predominantly (a), it may be that you have difficulty with the first of the two problems that we're going to look at, *blame*. Blame, in this context, means that, for you, the fault for things going wrong is located in the world outside of you. If I bump into you in the street, it's because I'm an idiot, or because I was deliberately trying to ruin your day. Please read on, but promise that you won't shout at me later.

If you answered predominantly (b), it may be that you have difficulty with the second of the two problems caused by that old Negative Command Centre, namely, *guilt*. Guilt in this context means that the reason things go wrong is because you are somehow not good enough in some way. If I bump into you on the street, it's because you were stupid enough to get in my way. Please read on, but don't take anything I say personally.

In which a friendly alien asks us an important question

Now, that was a short questionnaire and the examples given were quite simple. Although it may be true that many people would have selected alternative answers somewhere in the middle of the two responses, it is also true that for the majority of people, tendencies towards guilt and blame are quite strong. In fact, in society, they are almost seen as normal. This leads us onto Rule Number Three of Modern Living:

Guilt and blame are extremely common; they are also completely pointless unless they cause something to change

Problems with blame and guilt

Let me explain what I meant with Rule Number Three. Let's use as an example a person who loses his temper on a regular basis with his wife. It might be over the most trivial detail: she forgets to remind him about a social engagement, say, but he loses his temper and shouts and yells at her. Now let's assume that the husband blames his wife for this incident. It's all her fault. Why does she have to be so stupid? The end result:

a horrendous argument over nothing, warfare in the home and stale sandwiches for tea for the next few days but, most importantly, no solution to the problem.

Now let's assume that once our harried husband has lost his rag, he immediately apologises. He'll never do it again, he reassures his wife; he must have behaved that way because he is such a bad person. He blames himself completely, not only for this, but for all other past indiscretions. The end result: tears all round, peace reigns again but, most importantly, no solution to the problem.

This is the key difficulty with these examples of commands from the Negative Command Centre, which are so prevalent. They don't work.

Another significant problem with these commands is that they reduce the potential for change by inappropriately apportioning responsibility. Responsibility is a touchy topic these days. Politicians seem able to get away with all sorts of things, some fathers and mothers don't take responsibility for their children, and many would argue that the vast majority of us don't take responsibility for our planet. This state of affairs is by no means new, but is certainly more obvious

In which a friendly alien asks us an important question

than ever before. Not taking responsibility for something, or taking too much, can really hamper our attempts to change. Look at the effect blame and guilt have on responsibility.

Blame makes it always someone else's fault, so we never need to take responsibility for our problems; guilt makes it always our fault, so nobody else has the chance to take responsibility for their actions. Neither response solves the problem, and both actively inhibit the chance to change. Blame and Guilt only make sense as solutions if we make changes after the event. Let's have another look at our example and change the ending a little.

A husband has a row with his wife. He takes a deep breath and as calmly as he can, thinks about what has just happened. Either he decides that it shouldn't have happened and takes the responsibility for it never happening again, or he decides that his wife could have reacted more calmly and takes the responsibility to tell her, without blaming her.

In either case, something new is tried and we have a different ending to the scenario: either the husband keeps his temper under control, or there is a discussion about the effect his wife's

In which a friendly alien asks us an important question

behaviour is having on him. But too often the same scenarios end in the same way, if we follow commands from our Negative Command Centre. Being intelligent, rational beings, we then have to find a way to rationalise why we make such decisions. And for this, we become slaves to shoulds, musts and oughts.

Slaves to shoulds, musts and oughts

First of all, let us get a couple of things clear. Responsibility is not burden. Obligation is not martyrdom. OK?

Every day, we are told how we should behave. Not only do newspapers, advertisements and television inform us of the standards we should reach, but our own heads tell us what we should or should not be doing. (As an aside, does anyone else find it strange that in the back of magazines that tell us we should be happy with our bodies and love ourselves for what we are, there are several pages of adverts for corrective surgery? It's only me? Oh . . .) Now, as we have seen, this can be a good thing, for example, when a little voice inside our heads (the Voice of Reason) tells

In which a friendly alien asks us an important question

us we're driving too fast, that perhaps we should slow down or even stop using the car and take a bit of exercise; but it can also be bad if we listen to the wrong instructions. If we restrict our lives to living the way other people think is best for us, it is easy to become a slave to shoulds, musts and oughts.

These thoughts often go hand in hand with blame and guilt. For example, constantly telling yourself: I *should* be a better/girlfriend/boyfriend /person/parent; I *must* work harder/faster/more; I *should* do more for other people; I *ought* to be more sympathetic with my friends – all add up to feelings of *guilt*. Meanwhile, constant complaints, like: life shouldn't be this hard; people should listen to me more; the world shouldn't be this unfair; other people should be more considerate, do nothing but shift the blame onto someone else and away from us.

We can see again the connection between our thoughts, feelings and behaviour that we looked at in chapter two. Imagine what would happen if you were constantly telling yourself, I should do better? Could you ever be really happy, or would you always be failing to live up to your own impossibly high standards? Imagine if you spent your time thinking, why aren't people more respectful to me? It would be impossible for you ever to be satisfied with how the world was treating you. And as we have seen, both of these responses lead to the same outcome: we don't take responsibility for our actions in a way that allows us to change anything. Nothing changes! And just to make things even more complicated, there is another trick we like to employ: reading other people's minds.

Mind-reading

We saw in chapter two that problems arise when we try to predict the future, for example, when we think to ourselves "No-one will ever really understand me!" and then act, feel and think on the basis that this is going to be true forever. Similar problems arise when we try to read minds. This happens when we interpret someone else's behaviour and then act, feel and think on the basis that our interpretation is flawless. Now, the brain is actually quite good at mind-reading a lot of the time. If we see someone sitting in a park

In which a friendly alien asks us an important question

sobbing and repeatedly jumping up and down on a picture of their boyfriend, we would probably have enough evidence to feel justified in our assumption that this lady is having the odd teeny-tiny problem with affairs of the heart. Unfortunately, life is usually not this simple – and yet we proceed as if it were. Look at these examples:

A young man is out with his girlfriend in the pub. The girl is very quiet. He thinks:

Mind-reading: "She's thinking of her ex-boyfriend" or "She's bored with me".

Shoulds, musts, oughts: "She shouldn't treat me this way" or "I shouldn't be so boring".

Actual reason for event: Girlfriend has exams the next day.

Outcome: Row, or he pesters his girlfriend to tell him what's wrong with him.

An employee is having a review. Her boss does not mention her performance. She thinks:

Mind-reading: "He doesn't rate me", or "Nobody ever gives me the praise I deserve".

Shoulds, musts, oughts: "I should work

harder", or "He should notice me more; he doesn't respect me".

Actual reason for event: Boss is an idiot.

Outcome: Employee starts to make more mistakes at work because she is so tired, or employee starts to make more mistakes at work because she is so angry.

A mother is at home with her son who is having one of his more difficult days. She thinks:

Mind-reading: "My child hates me", or "He's doing all this on purpose".

Shoulds, musts, oughts: "I must be a better mother", or "He should notice my feelings".

Actual reason for event: Child is having one of their "difficult" days.

Outcome: Mother begins to allow the child to get away with things, or
Mother cracks down on every single transgression.

Now we can see how complex these patterns of thought can become and what powerful emotions can emerge from them. Every day,

In which a friendly alien asks us an important question

psychologists work with parents who tell them that they are terrible parents because they can't get their children to do everything they tell them. Employees get depressed because they think no one has noticed their performance. Relationships break up because one partner begins to act on the basis that the other is deliberately trying to make them feel bad. I have seen women screaming at their two-year-old sons and then turning round to tell me that their poor child is "deliberately winding them up". Let me ask you a quick question: Where is our evidence for thinking these thoughts and do they actually help?

What tangled webs we weave . . .

Hopefully, I have demonstrated that we often proceed with total confidence in situations where we are really in the dark, and behave in a way that if we told our friends how we had acted and why, they would be appalled. A great many interpersonal problems are caused by following the orders of the Negative Command Centre: interpreting, mind-reading, and generally getting a situation horribly wrong. Psychologists often

In which a friendly alien asks us an important question

divide some of these thinking errors into different groups (psychologists love to have things neatly ordered). If we look back at the examples quoted above, we can add another couple of classifications to our system.

Molehills to mountains

This type of problem occurs when, on the basis of a single incident, we automatically assume the worst. For example, our Romeo from a few paragraphs above thought that his relationship was in trouble because his girlfriend was quiet; the mother thought she was a failure because on this one occasion she couldn't get her child to be quiet. Psychologists sometimes refer to this as generalising from a single event.

Calling ourselves names

You may remember the childhood rhyme: "Sticks and stones may break my bones, but words will never hurt me". Yeah, right. Anyone who has ever been insulted knows how harmful words can be. But every day we often label ourselves with some

In which a friendly alien asks us an important question

of the cruellest epithets imaginable: "I'm such a terrible person", "I'm a terrible husband and father", "I'm such a loser – how could anyone be so stupid", and so on. What's worse, because these thoughts come from our own minds, we accept them as true instead of subjecting them to any from of inquiry. Think of the damage we are doing by constantly telling ourselves that we're idiots or that we're failing in everything that we do.

Thinking with the blinkers on and leaping to conclusions

It is a beautiful sunny Saturday and the birds are singing. After opening a letter from the taxman that informs you that they owe you money, you decide to spend the day at the beach. Remarkably, there are no other cars on the road except yours, and you arrive earlier than anticipated. The beach is virtually empty and you have no difficulty in finding a spot overlooking the slow and gentle waves, the sun warming your skin. You reach down into your bag to pull out your beach towel and realise that you have left it at home.

Now, if the first thought you have at this point

In which a friendly alien asks us an important question

is "well, that's just typical. My day is ruined", you probably have a tendency to think with the blinkers on. In other words, good things are selectively ignored and you concentrate only on the bad things. There is also a tendency to leap (not just jump) to conclusions. Instead of thinking "well, I'll just have to shell out for another awful multi-coloured beach towel", you immediately select the most damning and negative response.

Although I hope I have convinced you that we can be our own worst enemy, I don't want you to despair: don't feel hopeless. In the next chapter we'll look at what we can do about it.

Imagine this – you have been asked by a race of intergalactic aliens if one of their race can accompany you while you go about your typical day. The alien knows nothing about guilt, blame, or unhappiness because its species has only one rule – do what you think will make you happy as long as it doesn't harm anyone else. The alien is a bit baffled by the fact that you seem unhappy at work and his supersensitive hearing detects a steep rise in your pulse and a tightening of the throat when your boyfriend phones you. He (she

In which a friendly alien asks us an important question

---

or it – you can never be sure with aliens) listens to you complaining about your friends, about your relationship and about your family. He monitors you for the whole day and sees how tired and stressed you get. Then at the end of the day he pours you a glass of Venusian wine and politely asks you why you do the things you do every day, given that they seem to make you unhappy.

What do you say?

ANXIETY

Problems with anxiety are extremely common and take a variety of different forms. For simplicity's sake, we will view all the anxiety disorders as occurring when (OK, take a deep breath) – the human body and mind react inappropriately to a given stimulus in ways that cause a number of physical symptoms associated with stress, such as elevated pulse, sweaty palms, shallow breathing and palpitations. Some of the most common forms of anxiety disorders are:

Panic disorder
Here, a person reacts in a way associated with panic and can feel as if they are going to die, often due to a misinterpretation of physical symptoms.

Obsessional compulsive disorder (OCD)
With this condition, people suffer both from obsessions (thoughts that will not go away)

and compulsions (the need to carry out a certain act, often repeatedly). A common example is the person who believes that they will become infected with germs (the obsession) and so has to wash their hands 40 times a day (the compulsion)

Post traumatic stress disorder (PTSD)

Following a trauma, a person can suffer from reliving the event in their mind. This causes terrible anxiety and can lead to an avoidance of doing anything that might trigger off memories of the event.

Phobias

A phobia is a fear that is out of proportion with the stimulus and leads to avoidance of the feared stimulus. The fear is irrational and can be in many forms – agoraphobia (fear of being trapped), specific phobia (of, for example, spiders or rats) and social phobia (where a person can become terrified in certain social situations).

Most of the anxiety disorders are treatable and react well to systematic psychological therapies. Having an anxiety disorder does not mean that you are mad. Your doctor can refer you to the relevant mental health profession-al, should you need treatment. There are also some good self-help packages available.

Chapter Four

The Miracle of the Super-clean Tenner

In which we start to shape our lives, take responsibility and create a miracle or two

How to make a miracle

Having just condemned the habit that people fall into of basing their decisions on telepathy, let me prove what a hypocrite I am by trying a spot of telepathy on you, my good reader. I imagine by now that some of you might be thinking, "all these explanations for why I think in the way that I do are all well and good, but what exactly am I supposed to do about it?" Some of you might even be thinking one of those hard to resist but extremely counterproductive thoughts such as, "well, even if all that makes sense, I've

In which we start to shape our lives, take responsibility and create a miracle or two

been this way for ages – it's to late to change any of it now".

As you have been very patient with my attempts to explain why people do what they do, you deserve a treat. I'm going to ask you a question, which will introduce some language that we don't often hear in our beaten-down Negative-Command-Centre dominated world, the language of miracles, change, imagination and possibilities. Please turn down the volume on the Negative Command Centre and get ready to begin to explore.

Psychologists often call this the *Miracle Question*. It goes something like this . . .

You turn off your bedside lamp and get yourself comfortable in bed, ready to go to sleep. Within a few moments you begin to feel warm and relaxed and drift off into a peaceful slumber. You sleep soundly and wake feeling refreshed and ready for the coming events of the day. You suddenly notice that everything is subtly different. You climb out of bed feeling excited, a sense of wonder stirring in your mind. You realise that while you were sleeping, a miracle has taken place. Everything is how you would want it to be and you have been blessed with the life that you have always wanted.

In which we start to shape our lives, take responsibility and create a miracle or two

Now, close your eyes and ask yourself to imagine, in as much detail as possible, what the first thing is that you notice has changed?

For all of those of you who responded, "I'm a millionaire and Brad Pitt/Charlize Theron is lying in bed next to me", fair enough. It is quite probable that many of us would have similar fantasies. But this isn't a fantasy, it's a miracle – and whereas fantasies usually stay just as that, miracles do happen, every day. More importantly, they are within our reach.

Now we need a few rules so that we can better understand our miracle.

Start small

For most of us, waking up next to a movie star in our very own beach-side residence would be quite a drastic transformation. It is very difficult to imagine, realistically, what steps we would need to take to get from where we are now, to a position where we are hobnobbing with the rich and famous (although please don't let me put you off trying!). Instead, we are going to focus on things that are achievable now. So, take time

In which we start to shape our lives, take responsibility and create a miracle or two

to think about what the first small thing would be that you would notice.

Perhaps it would start with a feeling. Maybe you wouldn't feel tired or stressed or nervous about the day ahead. Perhaps you would be feeling more confident, more alert. Then again, perhaps it would be something you are doing. For example, you might dress in a different way, or wear different makeup. Or maybe, the first small change that you would notice is something that you are thinking . . . you might be thinking positive thoughts about yourself.

What is the exact nature of the change?

Be absolutely clear about what has happened. Describe it in as much detail as you possibly can and use as much positive language as you like. In this day and age, we are used to hearing and using in-depth descriptions of awful events, so why not treat yourself and imagine, in minute detail, something really pleasant happening?

How would you look if you were more confident? Perhaps you would stand taller, hold your head up higher. Maybe you would laugh more. What would be the first thing a friend or relative

In which we start to shape our lives, take responsibility and create a miracle or two

would notice about you that would tell them that something had changed for you? How would you describe the change to them?

What evidence do you have that the miracle is already happening?

Have there ever been moments in your life where you have felt/looked/thought like this? Try and ignore the commands coming from your Negative Command Centre that tell you that you've never been self-confident or assured. If you really can't remember such an occasion, don't worry – think of the moments in your life that most closely resembled feeling confident and assured.

Then ask yourself what you were doing when this little miracle happened? What were you thinking and feeling? What was happening for you at the time? What was special about this moment that made you feel so confident? How did people around you act when you felt that way?

The Miracle Question introduces the following ideas that we will look at throughout the rest of this book:

In which we start to shape our lives, take responsibility and create a miracle or two

- Changes happen all the time, but sometimes they are so small we don't notice. The simple mathematics of this is that if you add up a lot of very small changes you can start a revolution.
- Changes are within our power, but sometimes we need the necessary tools to help the process along.

There are two other points that lead on from the Miracle Question and that apply to the other techniques that are to come. Firstly, we need to retrain our minds to accept positive thoughts and this takes practise. And secondly, we can start making changes now.

Responsibility, doughnuts and bagels

Earlier in the book, we talked about responsibility and the effect that guilt and blame had on it. The more astute or pedantic among you will have noticed that I didn't actually define what responsibility was, so without further ado . . .

In which we start to shape our lives, take responsibility and create a miracle or two

Responsibility is accepting the consequences of our actions in such a way that we are able to build on successes and learn from failures.

In practical terms, this means that we start to create what psychologists sometimes call *Positive Feedback Loops*. For want of a better metaphor, I will call them *Happy Doughnuts*. We have already looked at what could be called a Negative Feedback Loop, or (to milk the food metaphor for all it is worth) a *Sour Bagel*, when we looked at the person who was shy when she went to a party. This feeling of shyness looped into thoughts that she was boring, which in turn looped into her behaviour changing for the worst and meant that she stayed at home and never went to parties. A Sour Bagel reduces our opportunities for change (and they generally taste lousy). A Happy Doughnut, on the other hand, looks something like this:

In which we start to shape our lives, take responsibility and create a miracle or two

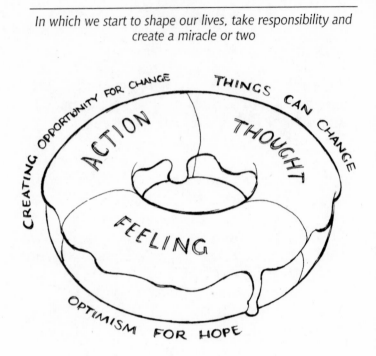

The 'happy doughnut'

Let me give you an example – let's return to our party-goer and see what happens when she allows the possibility of change to enter her life.

First of all, let us assume that she is going to take responsibility for what is happening to her. In doing so, she accepts the possibility of change and that she can be an active agent for change in her life rather than a passive recipient. The

In which we start to shape our lives, take responsibility and create a miracle or two

possibility for change engenders optimism and hope, rather than the despair that things will always be the same. This means that the volume on the Negative Command Centre is turned down. Our heroine now starts to look for different types of evidence. For example, on the basis of the Miracle Question she starts to look for small signs that she isn't as boring as she thought – perhaps things as small as someone saying hello to her at work for the first time. This, in turn, permits behavioural change: perhaps our heroine starts making small talk with people in shops. Just for 30 seconds or so every day, she starts to behave with the concept in mind that things can be different

This is a truncated example, but hopefully it highlights the fact that all meaningful change begins in a small way – even if you want to waken up next to Brad or Charlize, you have to first accept it is possible and then take small steps on the road to achieving your goal. Taking responsibility for both the steps that are successful as well as those that aren't means that your life will begin to happen under your control.

In which we start to shape our lives, take responsibility and create a miracle or two

Consequences revisited

In the last chapter, we looked at some of the consequences of following advice from the Negative Command Centre. We saw how it was possible to create situations where either we blamed ourselves for the consequences and assumed that we could never change, or we blamed others for the consequences and assumed that our situation would never change.

The end result was that many situations were never resolved. Many couples, for example, would admit that they have similar rows about similar things, over and over again, like a recurrent nightmare. People sometimes report that they feel that their lives are trapped in cycles that they feel powerless to break out of.

Now let us assume that a person does not revert to their default positions of guilt or blame when a difficult situation arises. Instead, they create situations where change can occur both from their own actions and from changes in the world around them.

How does a person do this? They change their default positions.

In which we start to shape our lives, take responsibility and create a miracle or two

Instead of immediately assuming that either they are at fault or everyone else is at fault, they look to see where change can come from. Perhaps they can do something differently, not because they are a bad person and because they must do better, but because a new way of doing things may be more effective.

Or perhaps they can promote change in their environment, maybe on a fairly simple level, such as asking someone not to smoke in their car, or on a more complex level by suggesting and helping to implement changes at work.

Critics and coaches

On a couple of occasions in the paragraphs above, I mentioned something called default positions. A default position is simply the state that a system (whether that system be a computer, a person or even a government) will resort to if there are no conflicting influences on it. For example, a man may tend toward a default position of eating too many cakes if his wife isn't around to tell him that he is putting on weight. A government may tend towards ever more terrible acts of dictatorship if

In which we start to shape our lives, take responsibility and create a miracle or two

there is no opposition. People who are slaves to shoulds, musts and oughts, who follow the advice of the Negative Command Centre, often have a default position that is similar to being ordered to jump through ever decreasing hoops by a fierce critic shouting from the sidelines:

"Oh, you never get anything right, do you! You're always making stupid mistakes! Why can't you, just for once, do something that isn't doomed to failure! Either you don't make any effort and you make a mess of it all, or you try too hard and people think you're an idiot!"

In which we start to shape our lives, take responsibility and create a miracle or two

Ouch. Imagine how unhelpful all that is. Now, wouldn't it be better to have a helpful, friendly person coaxing encouragement from the side-lines. Like a magician drawing a rabbit out of a hat, seemingly producing something out of thin air - but we all know that the rabbit is hiding in there somewhere don't we? We need positive thoughts to make miracles happen: "OK, let's take our time and think about this. What could we do that's different in this situation? What

In which we start to shape our lives, take responsibility and create a miracle or two

skills have we got that could turn this on its head? How about we try that and then maybe we could try this? Or even we could suggest that and then sit back and see what happens. . . well, there you go, I didn't expect that to happen, but it seems to have worked!"

What language are we speaking here?

Something that you may have noticed as we've been wending our merry way through all this information is the different types of language that we use when we follow the different instructions. For example, the language from the Negative Command Centre is often very harsh and critical, unbending and very black and white – it is either "this" or "that" and there is no room for grey areas, argument or change.

In contrast, the language of change is hopeful, optimistic and gentle. There is no room for blame or accusation because this style of thinking acknowledges that both are pointless unless something changes. It also recognises that there is no point in contemplating failure. Failure is just an emotionally loaded word that can make

In which we start to shape our lives, take responsibility and create a miracle or two

us feel bad about ourselves and our accomplishments. Instead, the language of change simply sees things that have worked to a greater or lesser degree in the past. Whichever way it adopts, new opportunities are created.

Still not convinced that there are viable alternatives to guilt and blame? OK, let's look at what we're giving up if we start to follow different commands.

What have guilt and self-blame ever done for us?

When people try to stop smoking, they often worry about all the things that they may have to give up, for example: their crutch, their support at times of stress, part of their self-image. Incredibly, for many people, these things outweigh the facts that when you stop smoking you improve your health, you gain (for the average smoker) £1500 pounds a year, you are more capable of exercise, your life expectancy increases, and so on. A classic argument from smokers regarding the health issue is "yes, but you've got to die of something". Sure, but why actively choose to do it in a slow, painful way from cigarettes?

In which we start to shape our lives, take responsibility and create a miracle or two

The same thinking often applies to people who want to make changes in the way that they think and behave. We've looked before at some of the things that people say to themselves to prevent change, things such as, "I've always been this way", "I'm too old to change now", "It's impossible. I'm just not the type of person who. . .". Now, just as a smoker needs to think carefully about what will change for them and their lives if they change their behaviour, so we all have to consider what we are giving up if we change the way we think. These may include:

- "The way I think and feel is familiar. It helps me makes sense of things." That's why we start on a small scale. Take each change a step at a time and go at your own pace. One of the great things about all this is that you don't have to feel as if you're being pressured and rushed.
- "If I change, people won't like me anymore." This is falling into the trap of taking responsibility for other people. If you change and certain friends find it hard to adjust, whose problem is it?
- "My family won't be able to cope if I decide to give up my job and go back to being a student."

In which we start to shape our lives, take responsibility and create a miracle or two

Have you asked them? Are their objections reasonable? Do you care? What's best for you – taking steps to have the life that you want, or allowing fears about other people's feelings to dictate what you can and cannot do?

- "I know guilt and blame don't really help me, but this is who I am." What a strange thing to take pride in. Why not take pride in the fact that you are happy and capable, instead of stricken with guilt?

Don't forget – if you try to change something and find that it doesn't work, you can always try something else. All I suggest to you is this: set yourself a goal and try and make small changes every day that take you closer to that goal. If, after a month, you feel that you were happier being the way you were – fine. Sell this book in a second-hand shop and choose the way you were living! You will have lost nothing by trying this experiment.

Now, I would like to invite you to the next chapter, where we'll take a look at some of the techniques that people can use to help them get closer to their goals.

In which we start to shape our lives, take responsibility and create a miracle or two

What is the miracle of the super-clean tenner?

Earlier in this chapter I claimed that not only do miracles happen, but they happen all the time. We just have to look for them in the right places and at the right times. For example, let us assume a man is trying to find a £10 note that he has borrowed from his girlfriend. He searches high and low for it, but can't find it. At this point, he could castigate himself for being so stupid, but he doesn't – he accepts it as just one of those things that happens. A few days later, our protagonist has forgotten all about the missing tenner. Putting his hands in the pockets of his recently machine-washed jeans, what should he find but the missing money, now incredibly clean, having miraculously managed to survive its 40° ordeal. Now, you may be saying to yourself, "well, that's not very miraculous". But – is it any less miraculous than opening the paper and finding an advertisement for just the right job? Is it any less miraculous than resolving an argument with a partner that has dragged on for years? My point is this – strange and quirky things happen every

In which we start to shape our lives, take responsibility and create a miracle or two

day, but sometimes we are too preoccupied to notice. The finding of the long-lost tenner becomes a miracle if we allow ourselves to notice all the strange and wonderful things that are going on around us and also if we allow ourselves to reframe the events of our lives.

DEPRESSION

Many mental-health professionals think of depression as the "common cold" of their job, as this disorder is so prevalent. Depression is characterised by extreme examples of the problems in the styles of thinking that we've been looking at. A person with depression typically has very negative thoughts about the following areas of their life:

• Themselves

People with depression often think very negatively about themselves, thoughts such as "I'm useless", "I can't cope" or "I'm a failure". This impacts on their feelings (sadness, misery and despair) and on their behaviour (restricted activities).

• Their world

People with depression often think that their world is a cruel and unfair place and that there is no hope for change. Thoughts such as "No-one cares about me" or "the world would be better off without me" mean those suffering from depression often do not engage with other people or with their world.

• **Their future**
Thoughts such as "it'll always be this way" or "I'll never get better" can dominate a depressive's thinking. This can impact on behaviour because they stop trying anything new.

Having read this far, you may be able to spot the thinking errors that a person with depression commits, for example, acting on thoughts without evidence, treating thoughts as if they were facts, black and white (either-or) thinking, self-blame and guilt. Depression can ruin lives but a variety of treatments, aimed at altering both behaviour and thought patterns are available. These Cognitive Behavioural Therapies (CBT) have proven to be especially effective. Consult your GP if you feel that you or someone close to you has a problem with depression – in the vast majority of cases, it is a condition that need not be with you forever.

INTERMISSION

Pocket summary for those, like me, with lousy memories

- Having problems has become more normal than not having problems. This is due to many factors, including the acceptance of the idea that life is and should be difficult.

- Many of us have an idea of what we would want our lives to be like, but find it very difficult to make the changes that are needed to achieve this.
- Surprisingly, a major factor in our inability to change things comes from ourselves and the internal voices that repeat instructions that we have gleaned from our experience that are not supported by sufficient evidence.
- We often treat these ideas as facts and use them to drive our behaviour, our thoughts and our feelings, often becoming slaves to shoulds, musts and oughts in the process.
- These ways of thinking often cause us difficulties when it comes to taking responsibility at the right times, and to dealing with the consequences of our thoughts, feelings and behaviour.
- We get so bound up in worrying that we stop noticing the little miracles that occur every day and concentrate instead on our perceived inability to change anything

But . . .

- If we are focused on what we want to change within ourselves and our lives (chapter one); if we are aware of the rules that we base our lives on, and whether they are helpful or not (chapters two and three); if we dispense with guilt and blame (chapters three and four); then we can begin to notice everyday little miracles, to start following the advice of a friendly, internal coach (instead of a harsh, internal critic) and begin building up positive instead of negative feedback loops.

Chapter Five

Stop, Be Still and Listen

In which we meet the Hunchback of Notre Dame

With apologies to Victor Hugo . . .

The Hunchback of Notre Dame is standing looking in the mirror one morning. He is feeling pretty pleased with himself after rescuing Esmeralda for the umpteenth time and is casting an appreciative glance at himself. He notices how powerful his frame is, how agile he has become, and nods in approval when he thinks of how his mind is as sharp as a razor, even if his speech is sometimes a little indistinct. He gives a quiet chuckle at all those times when he thought himself somehow inferior to everyone else – just because he looked different from other people – and realises that it is his very differences that make him special and unique.

In which we meet the Hunchback of Notre Dame

It has become easy in our modern world to get a number of definitions muddled up. We saw in chapter three how we sometimes confuse responsibility with burden and mistake obligation for martyrdom. It is also evident that we often imagine blaming other people, or ourselves, for something is somehow a resolution to a problem. Sometimes we make these mistakes because we follow messages from the Negative Command Centre or listen to harsh internal critics.

Now, in the example above, we see what the alternatives to these styles of thinking are. Quasimodo looks in the mirror and believes that he looks good today. He imagines that when he sees other people staring at him, they are noticing the same things that he is noticing: how powerful and agile he looks. This makes him feel happy and confident and, because he feels this way, he actually becomes more attractive to other people.

The point of this minor literary excursion is this – we often spend large portions of our lives collecting incomplete evidence to support false ideas that we are somehow bad people or that we are incapable of making change. But what would

In which we meet the Hunchback of Notre Dame

our lives be like if, instead, we collected evidence to suggest that we were good, attractive, intelligent people?

Some more cock-eyed definitions

I asked a large number of people the question above. Sometimes the answers I received illustrated how clearly the voice of the Negative Command Centre can control some of our actions. Many of the replies were along the lines of "People who think they're really good looking or attractive are so *egotistical*", or "I know someone who's always going on about how good things are going for them. They're so *arrogant*."

The words arrogant and egotistic have very negative connotations. They conjure up images of people walking around, lovingly preening themselves in every available mirror, criticising other people for not being as good as they are at certain things. I would tend to agree that such people are not particularly attractive – if you constantly feel that you are taking second place to someone else's ego when you are talking to them, it can be very unappealing.

In which we meet the Hunchback of Notre Dame

But unfortunately, these definitions are often applied far too widely and people even use them to rationalise why they are not making any changes to their lives, telling themselves "Oh, I'd hate to be that, cocky/egotistic/arrogant/full of myself".

Take the following dialogue as an example.

Bill: How are you doing today?

Richard: Fantastic, thanks, Bill. I'm feeling extremely positive about myself, and really enjoying what I'm doing. How are things with you?

Bill: Just great, thanks for asking. I've been doing a bit of exercise and that's making me feel good and I've gone back to doing a bit of painting at the weekends. It's something that I really missed doing, but because I've been working so hard, I just didn't have the time to do it.

Richard: That sounds great, Bill. You're really looking after yourself and doing things that you really enjoy. It'll be really good to catch up with you some time and you can tell me a bit more about what you're up to.

Bill: Thanks, Richard, that's good of you to say

In which we meet the Hunchback of Notre Dame

so. By the way, I've got to say – you're look-ing great at the moment! What have you been doing?

Richard: I've just been feeling good about my-self, recently. I used to feel guilty about not spending enough time with the kids and with Clare, but it didn't do me any good. So, we had a big long chat last month and decided I should drop a day at work, so that I've got a bit more free time.

Bill: Fantastic! It looks like it's really working out for you.

Richard: Cheers, Bill! You take care of yourself.

Now, would anyone describe Bill or Richard as being arrogant or egotistic? Would anyone say that they are somehow putting anyone else down with their attitude? Are they so busy thinking about themselves that they don't have time to listen to what other people are saying?

Now, let's listen to what might be described as a more "normal" conversation. Pay particular attention to the language that is used and the ef-fect that it has on you.

In which we meet the Hunchback of Notre Dame

Bill: How are you doing today?

Richard: Oh, you know. Getting by, I suppose. You?

Bill: Could be worse, I guess. How was your weekend?

Richard: Don't even ask. The kids were a nightmare and Clare's raging about the decorators cancelling for the second week in a row.

Bill: You never get a break, do you?

Richard: Nope. I'm just going through the motions at the moment. Anyway, how about you?

Bill: Oh, you know how it is. I work so hard during the week, Friday is just a night to collapse in front of the TV. Saturday, I get all those boring jobs done that I don't have time to do during the week and Sunday's spent getting ready for Monday again.

Richard: Makes you wonder why we bother, eh?

Bill: Sure does. Still, fancy a couple of beers on Wednesday night?

Richard: That'd be great. Don't let them get you down!

Bill: Huh! I'll try. Keep your chin up.

Which conversation is the more draining to hear? Which of these pairs would you prefer to

In which we meet the Hunchback of Notre Dame

spend time with? Why do we find it so difficult to answer the simple question "How are you?" with something positive? Is the position that Bill and Richard take in the second example any more valid and real that the position they take in the first?

Think of the language Bill and Richard use in the first example: positive, upbeat, full of new things and enthusiasm. How do you think their choice of language makes them feel? Now read the second example again – doesn't their choice of language make you feel old and tired? How do you think they feel?

The language that we use when we think and talk is terrifically important. It shapes everything around us. When children first learn to speak, they see everything that has four legs as "a doggie". So when they see a cat, or even a sheep, they still say "doggie". Now imagine a person, who frames everything with negative language, no matter what happens to them. This way of thinking is just as limited as a toddler's early speech.

Now, I want you to try an experiment for me. I want you to sit in front of a mirror for 10 minutes and tell yourself nothing but positive things.

In which we meet the Hunchback of Notre Dame

I would ask anyone whose immediate response is that it's a crazy or stupid thing to do, these simple questions – Yeah? And? So? What? So what if it's crazy? So what if it's dumb? Why not take the time to think nice things about yourself? What can you possibly lose? Why is sitting in front of a mirror and saying to ourselves "My God, I look old. Where have all those worry lines come from?" any more valid that sitting in front of a mirror and saying "For someone of my age, I'm looking really good! Those lines just show people I've lived. And look at that cheeky twinkle in my eyes! Fantastic!"

Now you might be tempted to say, "you've just spent 20-odd pages telling us we have to have some evidence for thinking certain thoughts. Well, where's your evidence that I'm a nice person?" Thank you. You've just brought me nicely back to the point I made earlier.

We spend a lot of time thinking we're terrible people based on the flimsiest of evidence. Why not begin to think that we're terrific people on the flimsiest of evidence?

In which we meet the Hunchback of Notre Dame

In other words, why put so much effort into looking for evidence that doesn't exist to support our theory that we are bad people, when the only effect it has is to make us feel miserable and prevent us from doing things? Why not use some of that energy thinking positive thoughts about ourselves? Who is more deluded – the person who just feels happy about themselves and their place in the world, without worrying about the evidence for it, or the person who goes round actively seeking evidence that suggests they are "bad"?

Reframing

Unfortunately, most of us have had a lot of practice in thinking that there's something wrong with us. From our interpretations of other people's comments, from our attempts at telepathy, from all the things that people have said to us over the years that we've harboured and put in a little file marked – don't forget, when we were 14, Jimmy Baxter told us we were fat and ugly, so we must be – it can now be quite a challenge to think in positive ways. Luckily enough, however,

In which we meet the Hunchback of Notre Dame

just as there are plenty of techniques that make things difficult for us – telepathy, making mountains out of molehills, and so on – there are plenty of techniques that can help us retrain our minds to think in a far more positive way and, in so doing, moving us closer towards whatever goals we might have.

Reframing is one such technique. It is simply the ability to talk back to ourselves when we find that we are leaping to conclusions. For example, let's contrast the thinking patterns behind the two approaches.

Situation: Your child gets a terrible report at school.

Leaping to conclusions: It's a complete disaster at the worst possible time. What am I going to do?

Reframing: Well, we thought there was a problem and this seems to be the proof. We need to have a word with the school and talk to little Jimmy too, so that we're all pulling together to do the right things.

Situation: It's the busiest time of year at work and you come down with the flu.

In which we meet the Hunchback of Notre Dame

Leaping to conclusions: Oh, no! I can't afford to be ill! I'll just have to carry on. This is going to kill me.

Reframing: This must be my body's way of telling me to slow down – I've been working so hard recently. Can't argue with my body though. I wonder if I can ask Mike to pick a few things up for me on his way home? I need to take it easy.

Situation: Your boss informs you that you have to work an extra shift.

Leaping to conclusions: Typical – people are always taking advantage of me.

Reframing: That's a pain, but I could do with the extra money. I guess it shows that my boss has some faith in me, too. At least if I need to take a day off next month to go and see my parents, I've more chance of being allowed to.

Situation: You don't get offered the job that you wanted.

Leaping to conclusions: I don't know why I bothered – I should have known I wouldn't get offered that job.

In which we meet the Hunchback of Notre Dame

Reframing: Damn. Well, where do we go from here? The letter says I was short-listed, so that's something, and it says that there might be another job coming up in a few months, so I could try for that. In the meantime . . .

Notice how leaping to the conclusions offered by the Negative Command Centre actually limits your options. The person who didn't get the job they wanted has nowhere to go after thinking "I don't know why I bothered". It is almost like following a film script – this type of response offers no room for improvisation or deviation from the plot, no hope of thinking anything different and inevitably is negative.

Now look at what happens when we Reframe:

- Reframing is action orientated, so rather than being trapped in a black and white way of thinking, lots of options are generated.
- It is guilt and blame-free.
- It is practical and defuses difficult situations by providing solutions instead of more problems.

In which we meet the Hunchback of Notre Dame

But it sounds so difficult . . .

Reframing and the other techniques are new skills to be learnt. It took time, after all, to be so highly skilled at thinking on the black side of things! Just because something is difficult, it is no reason not to begin. Remember, start small and build up – practise, practise, practise. Look at the examples below. What advice could we offer to a person in the following situations? Where is the silver lining that we can look for that will illuminate possible solutions to the dilemma instead of creating more problems, or, even worse, dead ends? See if your answers match mine. If they don't, don't worry – yours may well be better. The important thing is to generate solutions in the first place.

- An argument with a partner *becomes* a chance to reflect, an opportunity for change, an invitation to consider the future of the relationship.
- A falling out with a friend *becomes* a chance for a bit of breathing space, an opportunity to evaluate the friendship.
- An old heirloom getting broken *becomes* a

In which we meet the Hunchback of Notre Dame

chance to evaluate which material things we really want, an opportunity to clear some space

You get the idea.

It is important to remember the importance of practice in developing skills like these. Noticing and creating little miracles, trying to move your life in the direction that you want it to go in, changing the language that you use to describe situations and reframing, are like learning the grammar and vocabulary of a new language. You have to practise it as well as using it every day, so that it becomes automatic and easy. Just to get you started using these techniques, here are a few more ideas.

Goal set

Wishing you could be happier, more successful, or that you could wake up with Brad Pitt by your side in the morning, are long-term ambitions that are fine – but we must start small. What is your goal for today? Frame it in positive language. Try, "I will complete the following tasks at work

In which we meet the Hunchback of Notre Dame

today," rather than "I hope I don't screw anything up today!" Make your goal for today achievable and realistic and break it down into small steps. If your ambition is to change the world in a day, your goals will swiftly become jails.

Watch your language!

When you describe something to yourself or to someone else, what language do you use? Is it the language of *impossibility* "I'll never get all this done", or *probability* "Where shall I start?" Do you use the language of *change* "This could be a real challenge", or *defeat* "There's just too much to do". If you are using negative words such as – never, hopeless, too much, too tired – try translating it into something positive – soon, hopeful, enough. If your thoughts tend to trail off – Oh, no ... – put in a few exclamation marks – oh, yes!!

Be pointlessly happy

It appears we don't need an excuse to be miserable, yet being happy often seems to need extensive rationalisation. Why? It is all too easy to get

In which we meet the Hunchback of Notre Dame

out of touch with the things that make us happy, so easy, in fact, that we can even forget what they are. We should find something to be happy about every day. It doesn't have to be anything big. All you need to do is take time to be happy about something – *stop* what you are doing and thinking about, *be still* for a moment and *listen* – what can you hear? Perhaps it is the birds singing in the trees, a neighbour playing music, the sound of cars – there are a million different things that go on around us every day. Stop and listen to them for a while and take the time to notice all the things that we are lucky enough to experience. As Woody Allen once said: "Being alive is better than the alternative . . ."

WHAT HAPPENS TO OUR BRAINS WHEN WE THINK POSITIVELY?

Scientists have studied changes in brain structure for many years, looking at the brains of patients who suffer from depression and then comparing them to people who don't. One of the things they have discovered is that, on a simple level, thinking happy thoughts and adopting a positive attitude can be incredibly powerful. Some research has shown that cancer patients with a very positive outlook regarding their illness often have a better outcome, a greater life expectancy and a better quality of life than those patients who rail against the unfairness of it all. Happiness and the chemicals that are released in the brain when we feel happy, can offer protection against stress and against colds. People who report higher levels of happiness tend to have stronger social support networks and more rewarding jobs (although it is hard to know if the happiness comes first and the social support networks follow, or the other way round). Most people report that when they are happy – regardless of why – they feel more able to complete tasks, set and achieve realistic goals and enjoy interpersonal relationships. All of these emotions do seem to actually change the structure of the brain. It is as if you can prime and programme your brain for happiness.

Chapter Six

Imagination

In which we start to let things go

Meeting the monkeys

I hope that some interesting things have been happening to you if you have been trying some of the techniques that we have been looking at so far. Maybe you have noticed some little miracles that you weren't expecting. Perhaps you have surprised yourself with the realisation that your life is closer to being the way that you wanted it to be than you had thought. Have you worked out a plan for a particular goal? What is it you are trying to change? Which skills are going to be particularly useful?

Please be patient if you have been trying some different things but not experiencing to-tal and complete bliss. Any change takes time to implement and time to reap the results. The important things to bear in mind are:

- To identify the areas you want to change.
- To identify the skills which are going to help.
- To identify the steps you will need to take.
- To be patient.

Human beings and monkeys

Now, just to digress for a second (there is an interesting point arriving soon, I promise. . .). As you will know, the human species shares a great many genes with apes, chimps and monkeys. But there are two important things that set us apart from our hirsute relatives. The first thing is *language* – our brains happen to be far more able to cope with the demands of complex language than that of other animals. We have looked at some ways of using language to our advantage in chapter five.

Another way we differ is that our powers of *imagination* are significantly more developed. This is very important, because it means we are able to plan and adapt in advance for our futures.

Imagination

In which we start to let things go

In which we start to let things go

Now, I can hear some dissenting voices from the back saying "I don't have any sense of imagination", or "I don't like books, I don't like music and I don't like films. Don't start asking me to do anything clever with my imagination because it just won't work".

Now, the very fact that we are able to protest about a situation that hasn't happened yet reveals the presence of the imagination. If you are capable of telling me what you are going to be doing next week, then you have an imagination. If you're capable of telling me where you want to go on holiday next year and why, then you have an imagination. Everybody has an imagination, although this may be very highly developed in some and not so much in others (in the same way that some people are very skilled at using language and some aren't), but it is there. It is one of the things that sets us apart from our ancestors.

Now, how can we use this to our advantage?

Visualisation

Imagine that you are on a beach somewhere. Perhaps it is a place that you have been to on holiday

In which we start to let things go

or somewhere you have seen on television or in a magazine. You can see that the beach is covered with fine, golden sand and is warmed by a glorious sun. Azure blue waves lap gently against the shore as you lie down comfortably on the sand. You close your eyes, the warm sunshine plays over your skin, seeming to enter every fibre of your body, making you relax as you breathe deeply and calmly. Somewhere in the distance you can hear the song of a bird calling to its mate, the sound complimenting perfectly the gentle caress of the waves on the beach. Your body feels comfortable and relaxed and with every new breath you take you feel more and more content. Your mind is empty of troubles, aware only of the sensations of your body – the sounds around you, the smells of the warm summer air, the scent of sea salt and nearby summer flowers drifting towards you, the warm sand on your skin and the brush of a gentle breeze through your hair . . .

Now, how do you feel?

Ever since human beings have had the means to describe their environment, artists, writers, actors and musicians have used the technique of visualisation to convey their message and to create

In which we start to let things go

alternative states for their audiences to visit. Psychologists and other mental health professionals realised that this incredible talent, that we all share, is a powerful tool when used to help us achieve goals, improve our mood or alter our relationships.

Trouble-filled pasts and feared-for futures

Imagining the beach scenario above elicits a whole range of different reactions from people. Some give a little smile and say "it reminds me of the time Jim and I went to . . .", while for others, a deep state of relaxation can be reached. The point is this – just as we often use language to create worlds that are full of negative outcomes for ourselves, so many of us use our imaginations to create what psychologists sometimes call **trouble-filled pasts and feared-for futures**. Simply put, this means that when we think of our pasts, we see only awful incidents and problems, and because of this when we imagine our futures, all we see are negative outcomes.

Now, imagine if we used this incredible skill to create desired outcomes. There are many ways we can do this.

In which we start to let things go

Use all of your senses

In the example above, the picture that was created tried to emphasise the role of the different senses, the smell of the air, the feel of the beach and so on. Psychologists have shown that the more senses we use in any given situation, the more likely we are to remember it. So, whenever you use your imagination to create a vivid picture of an event, situation or desired outcome, try to use all of your senses.

Mental videos

Successful athletes and stage performers use their imagination to rehearse what they want to happen in a given situation. For example, musicians can be seen strumming imaginary guitars, playing an imaginary piano or even hitting imaginary drums. Such scenarios train our bodies and our brains to know what success feels like and because we can use all the five senses to reinforce this learning, it is more likely to be successful. Ask yourself, what is the situation you want to see in reality? Asking the boss for a raise? Asking

In which we start to let things go

someone out¿ Enjoying yourself at a party¿ Rehearse it in your imagination first.

If a picture paints a thousand words . . .

If you are old enough to remember the classic TV series The Fall and Rise of Reginald Perrin, you might remember that every time Reginald thought of his hated mother-in-law, he received a mental image of an enormous hippo wallowing in the mud. This image perfectly summed up his feelings and attitude towards his poor unsuspecting relative far more effectively than a verbal description. Now, as well as the associative learning that our brain is capable of (in other words, when we think of one situation, such as the beach, it brings with it a whole host of connected or associated images) it is also capable of using the language of metaphor and images (which is why things such as the Tarot cards are interesting to many people). Earlier on in the book, we used the metaphor of modern life being like a juggling act. What metaphors can you use that are helpful resources¿ There are all sorts in use every day: I feel like a million bucks,

In which we start to let things go

it feels like a dream come true. Which ones can you use that will be helpful?

Antidotes to stress and tension

At the beginning of this book, we looked at the effects that stress could have on us. Stress and tension can be helpful, as we noted, but too much can have a deleterious effect on pretty much everything we do. But if we use our imagination, it can help us to relax. In fact, whatever we want to do, being in the right state of mind before we do it is absolutely vital. Before we take a closer look at relaxation, try taking the quiz below to find out how good you are at relaxing.

Dr Dave's SuperFast™ relaxation quiz

Read the statements below and circle the response that fits you best

How often (in an average day) would you describe yourself as relaxed?

(1) Never
(2) Occasionally

In which we start to let things go

(3) Sometimes
(4) Often
(5) Always

How many different ways do you have of relaxing?
(1), (2), (3), (4) or (5)?

How many times a day do you hear yourself saying, "I must relax"?
(5) Never
(4) Occasionally
(3) Sometimes
(2) Often
(1) Always

How often do you get tension headaches?
(5) Never
(4) Occasionally
(3) Sometimes
(2) Often
(1) Always

In which we start to let things go

How often do you find it hard to sleep because you "can't turn your mind off"?

(5) Never
(4) Occasionally
(3) Sometimes
(2) Often
(1) Always

Does being unable to relax ever interfere with your everyday life?

(5) Never
(4) Occasionally
(3) Sometimes
(2) Often
(1) Always

How many cups of coffee do you drink in an average day?

(1) More than five
(2) Between four and five
(3) Between three and four
(4) Between two and three
(5) Less than two

In which we start to let things go

Do you ever use sleeping pills/drugs to help you sleep at night?

(5) Never
(4) Occasionally
(3) Sometimes
(2) Often
(1) Always

Do you find it difficult to get going with tasks because you don't know where to start?

(5) Never
(4) Occasionally
(3) Sometimes
(2) Often
(1) Always

Do you find it difficult to complete tasks because you worry the result won't be perfect?

(5) Never
(4) Occasionally
(3) Sometimes
(2) Often
(1) Always

Now add up your score.

In which we start to let things go

Are you Mr Chilled or Lady Anxious?

Once you've got your total, check your result with the scores below.

Between 40 and 50

My compliments to you, you are the kind of person who finds it easy to shut off and relax, who manages their workload effectively and doesn't let stress interfere too much with their lives. How do you manage it? What are your tricks?

Between 30 and 39

That's pretty good. Sometimes, stress gets on top of you, perhaps you get a few minor physical symptoms from time to time, but you seem to be able to prioritise what is important and keep a check on stress. What are the patterns to watch out for when you get too stressed? Perhaps there are some identifiable markers of stress for you or identifiable situations that get you a bit hot under the collar. You obviously have techniques that work to help you relax – how can you use these techniques in difficult situations? How can you adapt them to help you in others?

In which we start to let things go

Between 20 and 29

The stress of life sometimes affects you far more than you want it to. Perhaps you find yourself with headaches or stomach complaints or other niggling ailments – maybe you catch every cold going and then make yourself go back to work. It is good that you can be honest about how much stress there is in your life – what can you do about it? Now is the time to start taking some preventative steps to help combat the effects of stress.

Less than 19

It really is time to take stock. Physically – headaches, stomach complaints and sleep problems – the effects of stress are starting to be as troublesome as the thing that is stressing you itself. Do you need those cups of coffee to get you going in the morning? Are you starting to ruminate (spending time mulling things over in your mind) more than you're actively seeking practical solutions? **Please be careful** – it is going to be difficult to change things in the way that you want if you are too stressed to put any kind of plan into operation.

In which we start to let things go

Relaxation

Welcome to another skill!

Just as some people find it easier than others to learn things, some people find it easier than others to relax. Do not despair – anyone can pick up this skill with a bit of practice and application. It all depends on the amount of work you put in – don't give up after a couple of tries!

The physical symptoms of stress can all be eased through the use of various relaxation techniques. Tension headaches and stomach complaints, for example, are often caused because we tense the muscles in the neck, shoulders and abdomen. By relaxing our minds, we can help ourselves to sleep better and stop ruminating. Furthermore, the techniques we have talked about in the last three chapters are all easier to implement when we are relaxed. Now, although we'll look at techniques for relaxing the mind and the body separately, they are really one and the same – sound mind in a healthy body as the saying goes . . .

In which we start to let things go

Giving your relaxation muscles a workout

We often don't notice when we're showing the physical symptoms of stress until we get headaches or other associated problems. This is because, for many of us, we only notice how our body feels when something is wrong with it. How many of us wake up in the morning thinking "Boy, my body feels good today! My lower back is really relaxed". Not too many, I would think. It's more common to notice all the little niggling aches and pains that can accumulate when we are busy and overloading our bodies. So, just as we need to take time to isolate and eliminate negative thoughts in order to improve our mental wellbeing, so we need to try and isolate and eliminate negative somatic (physical) feelings.

Before we start, find out how it feels to be tense, then relaxed, but do it on purpose. Clench your jaw as tightly as you can for three seconds – 1, 2, 3 – then suddenly relax. Can you feel the difference? OK, now try this with your shoulders and neck. Tense the muscles up tight for three seconds – 1, 2, 3 – and then suddenly relax. Get used to recognising the difference between tension and relaxation.

OK, now try this programme at home . . .

Get the setting right

Think about where the best place is for you to relax. Don't choose the bed, you might fall asleep. Instead, choose somewhere comfortable like a favourite chair. Now think carefully about when the best time for you to relax is – ideally a time when you are as free from distraction as possible. Tell the people you live with that you need a bit of quiet time.

Start from the top . . .

Once you are sitting comfortably, close your eyes. Let your eyelids feel heavy, but for now, keep your mind sharp and awake. Imagine that a warm ray of light is playing over your body and highlighting all the different muscle groups. How does your jaw and forehead feel? These are the two sites that often reveal stress – a clenched jaw, a furrowed brow. Breathing at a steady rate, allow your jaw and your forehead to relax.

In which we start to let things go

Now move that ray of light down to your shoulders. Are they hunched up or hanging comfortably? Let your arms feel heavy, before letting the light come down to your arms and hands.

. . . and work down

Now you've relaxed your head, shoulders and arms, try moving down your body, muscle group by muscle group. For example, tense and then relax the muscles in your chest and then move down to your buttocks, legs and feet. Make sure that you play that warm light of awareness over each muscle group in your body.

This is a very simplified programme but the essential components are the basis for pretty much any kind of physical relaxation system you want to try. The key components are:

- Be aware of the difference between tensed muscle groups and relaxed ones.
- Take time to be aware of how your body feels and the areas in your body that need to feel more relaxed.

In which we start to let things go

- Practise! This is one of those things that you can do even at the bus stop. Tense your muscles, relax them, tense them and then relax. Do this when you are sitting at your computer. Is your back hunched up? Are your shoulders high and tight, instead of low and comfortable?
- Find out what makes your body feel comfortable. Some people report that wearing certain fabrics makes them feel tense, while others make them feel relaxed. Aromatherapy has had some amazing effects – give it a try. Most chemists now sell essential oils at very reasonable prices. Just as we focus on what makes our minds feel happy, we must also take time to assess the state of our bodies.

Taking our brains to the sauna

Now that we know how to relax our bodies in preparation for making some changes, let's give our brains the same treatment with these super-fast troubleshooting handy hints.

In which we start to let things go

Watch what fuel you put in the engine

Now clearly this is something that applies both to our minds and our bodies. If you put sugar in the engine of a Porsche it will run like my battered old banger used to when I forgot to check the oil. If you drink coffee or lots of cola before bedtime, forget sleep. To relax your mind, avoid stimulants.

Limit your worrying

Got something playing on your mind? Is it something that just can't be solved easily, even if you've tried? Don't try to solve it then. Allow yourself to worry about the problem for 15 minutes a day – and then put it to one side. Some things resolve on their own, but very few problems resolve because someone worried themselves into a frenzy.

Make progress

Few things can inhibit relaxation more than worrying that you're not getting anywhere with something. Use the reframing techniques we've looked at. Give your brain some positive messages.

In which we start to let things go

Take action

Take practical steps to ease your worried mind. Forgetting things? Make lists. Don't know where it's all going to end? Don't worry about the ending, worry about where you can start – remember, first things first. Write things down or draw a problem, so you can look at it from another perspective.

Talk to someone

Talking a problem over with someone can really help put the worries to bed. This doesn't mean making your problem someone else's (remember all the things we've talked about in terms of responsibility), it means actively encouraging different perspectives on your life. If you don't have anyone to talk to about a particular problem, then talk to an empty chair and imagine that a wise old advisor is sitting there. What would they say?

What can you do about it today?

Don't worry about what might happen a few months down the line at this moment. Worry

In which we start to let things go

about what you can do today. Make your worries practical rather than apocalyptic.

So now we are building up a little armoury of techniques and ideas that can help you prepare to change the way you view things, how you respond to things and how you feel about things. In the next chapter, we're going to concentrate on some problem solving advice for a critical area of our lives – relationships.

THERAPY

If you think that a problem that you have cannot be resolved either by yourself or by time, then perhaps you may want to consider getting some outside help. Please don't feel ashamed or embarrassed about this. That can be one of the biggest hindrances to improving how you feel. And don't think, "there are loads of people worse off than me . . . I should be stronger/better". Breaking the chains of shoulds, musts and oughts is part of the challenge.

Here are some general tips, should you seek out therapy

- Trust word of mouth more than an advertisement.
- If you decide to go private, look at the costs. If, on the other hand you want to stay in the NHS, be prepared for long waiting lists.
- What kind of therapy will work for you? Talk to the therapist if you can and see if you're

going to gel. Getting on with your therapist can be just as important as the techniques that the therapist uses.

- Beware of quacks – check the qualifications of your therapist with their governing body. If more people did this, there would be fewer therapists still in practice that have no right to be. Any therapist who refuses to tell you what their qualifications are or why they should be seeing you, may well be bad news. The therapist may genuinely mean well, but may also be simply not qualified to do the job

- Find out how long the therapy might last and how often review sessions will be built into the work so that you can review improvements.

- If a doctor recommends medication for a problem, ask what the alternatives might be. If you must take medication, be an informed patient – what are the side effects? How long should the course continue for?

- If you do start therapy but you feel uncomfortable with the therapist – leave.
- There are absolutely no therapies where it is appropriate for the therapist to enter into a physical, sexual or exploitative financial relationship with a patient. This is abuse and must be dealt with. If this happens, seek advice from your Citizens Advice Bureau or the police.
- Do your homework. Use the Internet to find out about all the therapies on offer or use the information later in this book as a starting point. Therapies that cost thousands of pounds so that you can swim with a whale, are not therapies. Therapies where the therapist moves into your house are not therapies.

Chapter Seven

Communication Matters

In which we learn lots of clever acronyms and get what we want from relationships

Relationships

Still with me? Fantastic. I assure you that the end of the book will be worth the wait.

OK. In the last few chapters we've looked at a lot of different techniques that can be used not only to improve our mood, but also to improve our chances of making things happen. Now, hopefully, you have had some success – you're aware of where some of our self-defeating thoughts come from and you've been able to take some steps to defeat them. Perhaps also, you've been able to set some achievable targets for yourself

*In which we learn lots of clever acronyms and get what
we want from relationships*

and you're feeling the thrill of change trembling
through your bones and sinews.

Or – perhaps you've been arguing with your
partner and are not sure what to do about it. If
so, welcome to chapter seven. Once again, you're
in the right place.

Relationships can be the cause of – and the
remedy for – many of life's difficulties. Relationships can also be the place where guilt and
blame can come to the surface and make things
very difficult for even the most loving couple.
Furthermore, the process can be gradual, sneak-
ing up on us when we're not looking, so that in
the space of a few months, we can go from being sure that this person is the one to make us
complete, to standing on the doorstep, suitcase
in hand.

Rescue remedies for the
romantically ropey

We have looked in previous chapters at the causes
and effects of guilt and blame and some of the errors that people make when trying to understand
others. There is one classic error so common that

In which we learn lots of clever acronyms and get what we want from relationships

*In which we learn lots of clever acronyms and get what
we want from relationships*

psychologists have called it the Fundamental Attribution Error (FAE). It goes something like this . . .

If I am rude and touchy with my boyfriend, it is because I have had a very difficult day at work and am under a lot of stress. If my boyfriend is rude and touchy with me, it is because he is a rude, touchy, and a typically insensitive brute who is deliberately trying to make my life difficult.

In other words, I attribute my behaviour to things external to me (that is, it is not my fault), but I attribute other people's behaviour to stable, internal causes (they are an insensitive idiot). Hopefully, this looks a bit familiar – it is a bit like when people try to mind-read. Now, we have some ideas about what to do with this when it simply concerns ourselves. But what do we do when there is another person involved?

Communication, not telepathy

Essentially, what we have looked at so far are different ways of communicating with

*In which we learn lots of clever acronyms and get what
we want from relationships*

ourselves: saying things such as "I'm a nice person", "What will I do today?", "that's a challenge, not an obstacle", and so on. We try not to jump to conclusions, to make mountains out of molehills or to blame ourselves. And exactly the same principles apply to relationships – the only difficulty is that because of the FAE, we have to guard against telepathy and faulty interpretations. With ourselves, if we *internalise* blame ("I'm a terrible person", and so on), we run the risk of making our own lives very difficult. If we *externalise* blame ("My boyfriend's an idiot") we run the risk of *demonising* our partners – and as Buffy the Vampire Slayer could attest, living with a demon can be very tricky.

So, what are the important facets of communication? Well, we're going to look at two in this chapter: what I mean when I say communication *matters* and the importance of *assertiveness*.

Communication matters

Rule 1 – Communication is not trying to win an argument.

In which we learn lots of clever acronyms and get what we want from relationships

Rule 2 – Communication is being honest, respectful and seeking a compromise.

Rule 3 – There are better ways to "clear the air" than throwing plates at a loved one.

Relationships need good communication in the same way that plants need water and light. It's that simple. Partners may be physically attracted to each other, intellectually matched and share common interests, but without good communication, the relationship is doomed. So, what are the components of good communication? Well, it must be:

Mutual

This means that when two partners talk, there is an exchange of information that is mutually beneficial – points are not scored off each other ("Yes, but you did . . ." countered by, "Yes but you did . . ."). Mutual communication means that partners are not playing 'One Up' or 'Top Trumps', throwing irrelevant detail into conversations about a partner's past misdemeanours.

*In which we learn lots of clever acronyms and get what
we want from relationships*

Attentive

It is simply awful being with someone who looks
bored when you talk to them. Attentive (or active) listening improves relationships because
people feel that what they have is valued and important and that they have someone that they
can tell anything to without fear of censure.

Tactile

Some people describe themselves as "not very
touchy-feely". Well, that doesn't mean that you
can't show affection with a kiss on the cheek
when you come in from work, a squeeze of the
hand if your partner is sad, a cup of soup and a
kind word if they are poorly. The tactile compo-
nent of a relationship shows a partner that you
care, that you are concerned for them and most
importantly, that you are close by.

Therapeutic

Now, I should qualify this by saying that your
partner should not be your therapist. What I mean

*In which we learn lots of clever acronyms and get what
we want from relationships*

is that communication with your partner should have a therapeutic effect – you should feel better when you talk to them and feel that there has been a soothing of the day's trials and tribulations.

Energising

In a similar way, communication between partners should be a reinvigorating experience. Why? Because you feel listened to by your partner and because you feel that there is an interested witness to your life.

Respectful

Respect is a critical ingredient to all successful communication. If one partner feels threatened or criticised, or somehow inferior to their partner, then it cannot possibly be a relationship of equals. It becomes a relationship with a significant power imbalance, where decisions are not made as a couple but rather dictated to from on high.

In which we learn lots of clever acronyms and get what we want from relationships

Sympathetic

Sympathy is not pity – rather, it is feeling like you have a cheering section in your corner, someone who you feel understands you as a person and is supportive in all that you try. It also means that they share your triumphs and pratfalls, mistakes and successes.

Put all these qualities together and you get my acronym (Communication) M-A-T-T-E-R-S. Try making up your own. This will help you to find out what is important to you as a person. Do it as a couple, and it can be revealing (if your letters are "V-I-T-A-L" and your partner's are "R-A-N-D-Y" then perhaps you have a bit of a mismatch . . .)

Now that we have an idea of what type of communication we want in our relationship, lets look at some way to put our acronym into practice. For this we need to look at *Assertiveness.*

Assertiveness – what it is and what it isn't

Read through the scenarios below. Is there anything there that rings a bell? How would you react in the same situations?

*In which we learn lots of clever acronyms and get what
we want from relationships*

One

Phil comes home from a hard day at work, tired and
hungry. Luckily, he knows that his girlfriend Sarah,
has promised him a fantastic meal, massage and
video to help him relax, knowing that he has an
important day tomorrow. Phil is 20 minutes late,
caught in the heavy rush-hour traffic. When he gets
in, there is no sign of Sarah or the promised night
of luxury. Instead, he finds a short note: You were
late. Went to play volleyball with the girls. Phil tries
to call Sarah, but there is no answer on her mobile.
He waits patiently for an hour and then decides to
order a pizza and turn in for the night. At one in the
morning there is still no sign of Sarah. Finally, she
comes in, drunk and noisy with a couple of friends.
Phil goes downstairs to ask them to make less noise.
"You know I've got a big day tomorrow," he says,
quietly. Sarah giggles and Phil goes back up to bed.

What would you have done?

Two

Liza and Robert are on their first holiday together
for two years. They've managed to afford a B&B

*In which we learn lots of clever acronyms and get what
we want from relationships*

for the weekend and are really looking forward to it. On arrival they find that the double room with bath is actually a double room without bath – none of the three rooms in the small B&B have a private bathroom. Liza explodes at the surprised B&B owner while Robert looks on embarrassed.

What would you have done?

Three

Barbara and Colin are standing looking at their 10-year-old son who is bawling his eyes out because no one came to pick him up after football practice. Both Barbara and Colin are sure that it was the other person's responsibility to pick their son up. This is how their initial conversation goes:

Barbara: "Let's not fight about it now. Let's get Jimmy washed and cleaned up first."

Colin: "I'm sure I told you I couldn't make it because I had to go into school."

Barbara: "It doesn't matter now. Let's talk about it later."

Colin nods and then both tend to their son.

What would you have done?

In which we learn lots of clever acronyms and get what we want from relationships

In the first case – that of Phil and Sarah – we have an example of a style of communication called *passivity*. A passive response is one in which a person does not stand up for their own feelings or rights and finds it difficult to express their wants and needs. They shy away from confrontation and often describe themselves as people who "don't make waves". It is similar to the state of guilt – a passive person often locates fault within themselves and hopes, against hope, that people will one day treat them better.

In Liza and Robert's case, however, we have an example of a style of communication called *aggression*. An aggressive response is one in which a person lashes out against any perceived transgression – aggressive people are often proud that "they don't take any messing about from anyone". Aggressive people don't shy away from conflict and often see fault in everything and everyone, similar to the state of Blame.

Now, the problem with both of these responses occurring in relationships is that they actively invite mind-reading on the part of their partners, which, as we know, invites trouble. In the first case, it is hard to know what the wants and

*In which we learn lots of clever acronyms and get what
we want from relationships*

feelings of the passive person are, because they don't express them. In the second, it is hard to know what the wants and feelings of the aggressive person are, because they are couched in such confrontational terms. Those who have relationships with passive people often find it difficult to respect them, because their partner seems at the mercy of life. On the other hand, it is hard to respect aggressive people because you are always in a position of having to anticipate situations that may lead to a 'blow up'.

In the last case, that of Barbara and Colin, we have an example of an *Assertive* response to a situation. Neither adult seeks to score points off each other – the problem is not so important that it requires them to stand and have a fight in front of their son, but it is not ignored and left to fester, as might happen in a passive response. The problem is dealt with (their son is cheered up) and both adults agree to discuss the problem later.

*In which we learn lots of clever acronyms and get what
we want from relationships*

Comparing aggression, passivity and assertiveness

Time for another quiz . . .

*You are on a date with your boyfriend. You are giv-
en a substandard meal in a restaurant. The waiter
asks you if you are enjoying your meal. You . . .*

(a) Do not make eye contact with the waiter.
    You nod and mumble that the meal is OK.

(b) Look the waiter in the eye and tell him
    calmly that the meal isn't acceptable and
    you would like a replacement.

(c) Stare at the waiter with obvious hostility.
    You demand a replacement in a loud voice
    and make sure everyone else in the restau-
    rant knows how aggrieved you feel.

*Your girlfriend phones up at the last minute to cancel
a date that you have been looking forward to for
days. You . . .*

(a) Quietly and sadly say, "That's alright. I'm
    sure you've got better things to do."

(b) Express that you are disappointed, but ac-
    cept what has happened. You arrange to
    make another date.

*In which we learn lots of clever acronyms and get what
we want from relationships*

(c) Demand to know why this has happened
and make sure that your girlfriend knows
that this is the fourth time in as many
months that she has cancelled.

*You are discussing babysitting arrangements for the
next few days with your partner. Both of you have
an arrangement you would really like to keep. After
discussing it, you feel . . .*

(a) Sad, but you suppose your partner's engagement is more important than yours.
(b) Fine. It's his turn this week to go out and
yours the next.
(c) A sense of triumph. How dare he and his
friends think that their football match is as
important as your girls' night out?

*The alien we met in chapter three has come to visit
you again. This time, it has picked up quite a lot of language. It witnesses a disagreement between you and
your partner. The alien likens what it has seen to . . .*

(a) An ant letting itself be stepped on.
(b) Two ants carrying a leaf together.
(c) Someone stepping on an ant.

*In which we learn lots of clever acronyms and get what
we want from relationships*

By this time, I imagine you're getting pretty good at quizzes! Psychologists refer to something called *practice effects* – the more questionnaires and quizzes people take, the better they are at producing a result that makes them look good. I hope that you're still responding honestly – after all, you're the only person who's going to see the results.

I imagine that you can tell already the differences between the Passive response in (a), the Assertive response in (b) and the Aggressive response in (c). These examples also highlight particular differences between the three different responses.

Body language

Passive people tend to adopt a rather cowed, cringing appearance, as though they are expecting to be slapped for their impertinence at any time. They make eye contact in such a way that they are always looking up at their partner, as though acknowledging their inferiority. They tend to hunch their shoulders up, to make themselves look smaller and wring their hands.

Aggressive people often look like prize fighters limbering up. They stare at their soon-to-be-victim

In which we learn lots of clever acronyms and get what we want from relationships

as if challenging them to disagree. They often fold their arms and move quite close to their partner, as if challenging them to take a backwards step. Often, they lift their heads, as though sneering at the other person and try to manoeuvre themselves into a position where they can look down on their partner.

Assertive people are in the middle. They make eye contact to express interest, not aggression, they stand up straight because they are not people who others take advantage of. Their body language is open and honest and they often use simple, nonverbal communication, with nods, hand gestures, and so on, to indicate that they are listening.

Verbal communication

Passive people tend to talk in small voices as though embarrassed by what they have to say. Their conversations are often full of comments such as, "I'm sorry to have troubled you", "I know this is my fault". Their speech is often faltering and punctuated by pauses.

Aggressive people tend to shout, speak very quickly and not give the other person time to

*In which we learn lots of clever acronyms and get what
we want from relationships*

respond. Their conversations are often littered with "Now, what are you going to do about it?", "I've had it up to here with your. . .".

Assertive people tend not to raise their voices. They speak simply and clearly and actively listen when their partner has something to say. Their conversations are full of "I" statements – "I felt this when you did that," and "we" statements – "What can we do to change this/improve that?"

Emotional impact on partners

The partners of passive people often report feeling frustrated and angry with their partner's perceived apathy. They often resent their partner's refusal to take responsibility for things in the relationship and say of them, "I wish they'd just . . ."

Partners of aggressive people often report feeling scared or worried when they have to bring an issue up. They fear their partner's response and say that it inhibits ease of communication. They often resent their partner's inability to take responsibility for their behaviour and often say of them, "I wish they'd just. . . ."

Partners of assertive people feel able to talk

*In which we learn lots of clever acronyms and get what
we want from relationships*

about virtually anything with their partner.
They don't feel inhibited or angry, but describe
the mutual problem-solving as being reassuring.
They feel that they are really in a partnership,
which tries its best to come to a logical solution
about a problem.

And this, of course, leads on to the last point.
Aggressive and Passive responses do not solve the
problem.

Being assertive

So far in this chapter, we have looked at the components of successful relationships and some of
the different styles that people employ in relationships, in the hope of effecting changes. Now,
for homework today, I want you to try these assertive techniques.

Say it with your body

Psychologists believe that a huge amount of information is conveyed without any words at all.
Assertive people instinctively realise this. They
make steady eye contact, they stand up straight

In which we learn lots of clever acronyms and get what we want from relationships

when they make a request and they use gestures and open body language (they don't cross their arms, clench their jaws and their fists and look like they're about to go in the ring with Muhammad Ali). Just as relaxation, visualisation and positive thinking are the key precursors to effecting change, so too is body language the first step to being assertive in a relationship. Practise what you want to say in front of a mirror and make sure that you can look yourself in the face.

Say it with words

Assertive people don't blame. They use "I" statements, "I think that . . .", "I feel that. . .". They make clear logical statements and they don't need to raise their voice. If they are dealing with someone who is unreasonable, they employ something called the *Broken Record Technique,* which goes something like this . . .

"Yes, I understand that Jimmy has been getting into fights. I understand that you're upset. What I think we need to talk about is what we're all going to do about it."

"Yes, I can see that you're upset. But, again,

*In which we learn lots of clever acronyms and get what
we want from relationships*

I think what is important is that we talk about what we're going to do about it . . ."

"You're right. He shouldn't have done that. What do you think we should do about it?"

In other words, they keep repeating what they want to say until they are heard. This can be especially effective with children – "Yes, I know you want to stay up until three in the morning, but I said no", "Yes, I know you think it is unfair, but I have said no", "Yes, I know you hate me and I'm sorry you feel that way. But I have still said no". Don't back down if you think you need to say something, but don't be obdurate – the point is to make yourself heard, not to win an argument. Assertive people aren't particularly bothered about always being right.

Say it with your feelings

Assertive people make their partners feel validated and understood. They make their partners feel as if they are being listened to and they make their partners feel respected. How? By being clear, to the point, respectful, actively listening and not scoring points.

*In which we learn lots of clever acronyms and get what
we want from relationships*

Now, permit me a moment or two of mind-reading. There has been a lot of information to absorb in this and previous chapters. Although making a decision to change how things are in your life is simply that – a matter of choice – sometimes the results take a little bit longer to materialise. Don't worry if things don't happen straight away. Be patient and give all those seeds you've been planting a chance to grow. No one should feel disillusioned if they begin to learn a new language and are not fluent within a few hours; no one should feel disillusioned if they pick up a guitar and can't play like Eric Clapton after a few lessons. Now, with that inspiring message ringing in your ears, see you in Chapter Eight – don't forget to take all your personal possessions with you.

DOMESTIC VIOLENCE

Domestic violence affects thousands upon thousands of people every year – men as well as women. It also has consequences for the children who witness it. Domestic violence can be seen as an extreme distortion of the aggressive relationship style – problems are 'solved' by the use of violence. Violence can take many forms, not merely physical, but also psychological and emotional. Years of being told you're worthless, stupid, a failure, can have devastating effects on someone's self-esteem and self-worth, which of course, then makes it harder for that person to leave. It is the most vicious of vicious cycles.

Let me state the obvious – there is never, ever an excuse for physical violence in a relationship. I have heard people tell me, "He hits me because his parents used to hit him", "He screams at me because his parents screamed at him" – so what?

This is an explanation, not an excuse.

Hiding behind something that happened 30 years ago is not an excuse for physically/psychologically injuring someone else. Furthermore, saying "I know he'll change if I stay with him long enough" is a bit like saying "I know he'll see the error of his ways if we put him in prison for long enough". There is absolutely no evidence to suggest that this is the case, in fact, evidence suggests the absolute opposite: domestic violence spirals into progressively worse abuse.

If you know someone who is suffering from abuse, or are a victim yourself, do not accept it. It is not OK and it never has been. There is help out there if you look for it. Phone one of the many helplines or get in touch with the Citizens Advice Bureau to check out your rights. There are many organisations that can offer practical as well as emotional help.

Chapter Eight

Troubleshooting Off Days

In which we learn the difference between being patient and prevaricating

In the proceeding pages we have talked about a variety of techniques and ways of thinking that are designed to help us with a range of different situations and problems. Some of them will be more helpful to you than others and some will be more helpful in certain situations than others. What is important is that you now have a little battery of things that can help you in your everyday life. I'll summarise these later, so we all know we're singing from the same hymn sheet.

One of the things that you will have encountered, I'm sure, is that no matter how cheery you're feeling, no matter how positive your outlook and how carefully you reframe things, you

In which we learn the difference between being patient and prevaricating

will still have Off Days. An Off Day is simply that – one of those days where nothing seems to quite click, where nothing quite seems to flow. They can be frustrating and annoying and even demoralising. Well, never fear – here's what to do when they happen.

Why do we have Off Days?

After many years of training and working as a psychologist and having seen hundreds of patients, I can confidently assert that I still have no idea why we have off days. I do know that everybody has them and the triggers for them are all completely different. Sometimes, it's because we have too much to do, or even too little to do. Some people say it's because we "got out of bed on the wrong side", but often it's because, no matter how hard we try, we can't seem to shake off a feeling of being 'flat'. If you've followed some of the advice so far, you might be thinking "Hang on, I thought I was supposed to be feeling happier, and yet, just today, I feel lousy". Please don't throw the book out of the window just yet.

Firstly – relax, take a deep breath. The most

*In which we learn the difference between being
patient and prevaricating*

In which we learn the difference between being patient and prevaricating

important thing to remember with Off Days is that they don't go on forever. There are things we can do to ease them and create the preconditions necessary to feeling happier again. Let's look at some common situations where Off Days can really throw us and consider what to do about them.

Diet and fitness

Diet and Fitness have become more and more important in recent years and the awareness of how important they are has been a huge public health boon. But they have also become two more sticks to beat ourselves with on an Off Day. Look at some of these sample thoughts:

- I've ruined my diet with that burger.
- If I don't lose a stone in the next month, I'm a failure.
- I should be doing twice as much exercise as I am.
- I'll never find the time to work out . . . why bother starting?
- I just can't be bothered.

In which we learn the difference between being patient and prevaricating

Now hopefully, you're way ahead of me and can spot the antidotes to thoughts such as these. On an Off Day, though, the Voice of Reason tends to go on vacation. So, if you've decided to go on a diet or take up some exercise but you're having an Off Day, try this . . .

Look at the big picture

If you've set yourself a goal – say to lose a certain amount of weight within a certain amount of time or to achieve a certain level of fitness – firstly, look at whether your goal is reasonable. If the last exercise you did was 15 years ago at school, expecting to be able to run a marathon after two weeks' training is probably stretching it a bit. Next, look at where you are in terms of progress towards that goal. Don't look at how far you've got to go before you have a body like a supermodel; look at how far you've come. If today is the first day of your new diet/fitness regimen and you're wondering why you bothered, think back to your goal. Actually taking the trouble to set such a goal is a huge first step.

*In which we learn the difference between being
patient and prevaricating*

Temptation and prevarication

If that double chocolate-chip with extra chocolate bun is looking really tempting right now, use your imagination – how will you feel if you eat it? How will you feel if you don't eat it? If today is the first day you're going to brave the swimming pool but you're having an Off Day, ask yourself this – if you go today, even though you're having an Off Day, will it make it easier to go the next time or harder? If you decide not to go and stay at home instead, will it make it easier or harder to go the next time? Finally, don't beat yourself up. Calm down and consider if today is perhaps just not the right day to start a new project. This does happen sometimes – set a new date to begin. If you find that you've set yourself three or four new dates to start and something keeps cropping up, be honest – are you just looking for excuses? Go back to your goal – re-evaluate it and make sure that there's no excuse next time.

Smoking

Stopping smoking is simply the fastest way to improved health there is available. Within hours of

---

*In which we learn the difference between being
patient and prevaricating*

stopping, you're health is medically measurably better. You know all the benefits, you know all the risks, but today, you're having an Off Day. . . .

Start small

Is the idea of never having a cigarette again driving you crazy? Don't think about it then. Worry about the first hour; then the next hour. After 15 hours, it's time for bed and you've made it through the first day. Congratulations – you're well on the way. Now, having been a smoker myself, I know the little webs of intrigue that smokers use to keep smoking:

- I'll stop when I'm feeling a bit less stressed.
- I'll cut down gradually.
- I'll stop when cigarettes cost £10 a pack.
- You've got to do die of something.
- It's going to be horrible. I just can't face it today.

Can you see the flaws in these patterns of thinking? There will never be a perfect day to stop smoking. The first day will be tricky, because you're letting go off a habit. You've got to die of

185

*In which we learn the difference between being
patient and prevaricating*

something? True – non-smokers do die every day.
But why ruin your health on purpose? You're
having an Off Day, that's all – stopping smoking
is still one of the best things you can do for yourself. Go back to your plan. Before stopping, make
a list of the situations you're going to find difficult and work out a solution to them before you
begin. Enlist the support of friends. Don't put it
off until tomorrow, because it might be too late.

The late great comedian Bill Hicks summed it
up perfectly when he said "I've decided to stop
gradually. First, I'm going to lose one lung . . ."
Don't let a bad day put you off – take the plunge.

Coping with a broken heart

Off Days are very common after a relationship
breaks up or when you have suffered a bereavement. At times like those, the one and only rule
is this – *be very, very gentle with yourself*. It's going
to be difficult to get through this period. Accept
this and carry on. You will have days where you
wonder where the strength to go on is going to
come from. Accept this and carry on. You will
have days where you think that you're not going

*In which we learn the difference between being
patient and prevaricating*

to make it and you're never going to feel better.
Accept this and carry on.

If you remember the metaphor of the juggler
way back in chapter one, dealing with a break-
up or bereavement (and really, they're the same
thing) is a perfect example of this in action. You
can be sad, but allow yourself to hope. You can
mourn, but allow yourself to laugh.

Don't rush

The temptation after a bereavement can be to
wonder when it's all going to get better and
having an Off Day can really bring that into focus. There is no easy answer. We know that we
can't predict the future, but one of the keys to
recovery is to allow it all to happen. Recovery
is a process that happens in different stages at
different times for different people. A bereavement doesn't mean that you have lost everything – there is still you, the core of what you
are. Even though this may have been shaken, it's
still there. In time, you will remember this and
be able to move on. Don't let an Off Day cause
you to doubt yourself. Take your time.

*In which we learn the difference between being
patient and prevaricating*

Retirement and unemployment

Losing our job, whether voluntarily or involuntarily, can be very stressful and difficult. For many people, it is one of those situations where you don't know how you're gong to react until it happens. When we have an Off Day, it is not uncommon to think:

- Well, that's it then. It's all downhill from here.
- I'm useless.
- How am I going to cope?
- What will my family do?

These are huge questions that will not be solved by worrying about them 24 hours a day. Beware of generalisations – as we saw earlier on in the book, a job is an important part of who we are, but it isn't the only part. What can we do now that the worst has happened? Now that our lives have changed, do we look on it as an ending or a beginning? Who can we turn to for advice or help? What are we going to do today to help with the problem, rather than trying to seek a resolution to it all in one go?

In which we learn the difference between being patient and prevaricating

Parenting

Believe it or not, parents are human beings too! Off Days are common as a parent. There are always a million and one different things to do and there seems to be a universal law that on the one day when you really don't have the time or the space for anything else, something happens that you just have to act on: your beloved son throws up in the back of the car and despite being late for work, you have to stop to clean up the mess and return home to get him a change of clothes. Yum, doughnuts . . .

Now, just because you are having an Off Day, don't let any of the following thoughts add to the problems:

- I'm a terrible parent.
- She's doing it on purpose.
- Why isn't my partner doing more to help?
- My sister's got kids and they don't do that.

Again, I'm sure you can spot the thinking errors in the above statements: generalising, FAE, mind-reading. This is why it's important to practise all

*In which we learn the difference between being
patient and prevaricating*

the different skills we've been looking at, so that
they become second nature to us and we can address the issues that come up, even on an Off Day.
If you're having an Off Day, take a deep breath.
It will be easier tomorrow. Accept the fact that
every parent gets pushed to the limit by their
children from time to time.

But remember that – as difficult as it can be
at times –it is important not to blame or lash
out at the child. This will not solve the problem.
Children have Off Days, just as adults do. Don't
make any grand interpretations from your children's Off Days – it doesn't mean that they hate
you or that you're a terrible parent. It means, like
you, they're having a bad day. Try having some
fun together, do something enjoyable together,
take the strain out of parenting with a couple of
judiciously placed ice creams and crayons. Take
some time off, where possible, and where it isn't
possible, try and solve the problem of where you
can find help. There is help available to parents,
although sometimes you have to shout for it.

*In which we learn the difference between being
patient and prevaricating*

Coping techniques

The techniques and ideas outlined in this book
will help you on good days and bad, but there are
a few particular points to remember when you're
trying to cope with the Off Day blues:

It won't last forever

Bad moods and Off Days pass. Learn how to juggle and roll with the blows.

Be specific and don't generalise

Remember, it is just the problem in front of you
that you have to solve. Don't multiply it out of
all proportion. One bad day doesn't mean that
you've made the wrong decision to stop smoking, nor does it mean that you will never get over
the loss of a loved one.

Things aren't black and white

It's easy to think that we've run out of options
when we have bad days, but this is just a symptom of how you're feeling. There are always options. Bad days invite you to forget them, but
don't listen.

*In which we learn the difference between being
patient and prevaricating*

Take your time but don't procrastinate

Be honest with yourself. We all know the difference. How many times do we really need to sharpen that pencil before we start writing that letter? However, there is a bit of juggling to be done – we have to realise our limits and not push ourselves too hard, but also acknowledge when we are using "I'm having an Off Day" as an excuse to put something off.

OK? I hope you found that useful. Please don't be put off if you didn't – there's some great stuff still to come. . . .

DIFFERENT STYLES OF THERAPY

We took a brief look in chapter six at some of the things to look out for if you were considering beginning therapy. Now, it's time to consider some of the different types of therapy that are on offer. Before we have a quick tour around 'Therapyworld', let me reiterate two very important points. Firstly, there is absolutely no shame attached to seeking out therapy; the shame is in not doing anything about a problem you know you can act on.

Secondly, there are no therapies in which it is appropriate for a therapist to take advantage of a patient, be it physically, sexually or financially. In this event, the therapist should be reported to their governing body and if necessary, the police.

There are several things you will have to decide on if choosing to seek therapy. First of all, ask yourself which type of therapy would be the most appropriate for your situation? Seeing a therapist on your own for individual therapy, with a partner in couple therapy, or with your whole family – family therapy?

Many psychologists who read this will no doubt claim that the different types of therapy all overlap. This is more or less true, but cognitive therapies tend to focus on changing the thoughts that underly the behaviours, behavioural therapies focus on changing the behaviour, whilst the more psychoanalytic therapies focus on an understanding of where the problem comes from. psychoanalysis can be very long and time consuming and is not for everyone, while the more cognitive and behavioural therapies tend to be more practical. Possibly the most popular form of therapy on offer is a blend of the cognitive and the behavioural, cunningly termed cognitive behavioural therapy.

A more recent innovation in therapy has been the so-called "brief solution focussed therapies". As the name suggests, they tend to be very rapid and very much focussed on the patient accepting responsibility for their recovery.

There are also therapies that use the media of art, music or drama; therapies for children involving play, hypnotherapies, gestalt therapies (which blend ideas of hypnotherapy and hypnosis) and others. If you want to find out more try the internet, or ask your GP.

Chapter Nine

Let's Go a Bit Crazy

In which we learn a thing or two from eight-year-olds

When I was eight, my mother decided I should take piano lessons. This is something I will always be eternally grateful to her for, but at the time it made me react a little bit like someone who is scared of heights would if they were being forced to do a bungee jump.

After a few weeks of playing one-finger compositions, I decided to throw one of my trademark strops and had a tantrum in the middle of my lesson. My teacher, a rather intimidating woman called Miss Myerhoff, who was as deaf as a post but could tell from 50 feet away if I'd played a note with the wrong finger, calmed me down, sat me down next to her at the piano and began to play the third movement of Beethoven's

In which we learn a thing or two from eight-year-olds

Moonlight Sonata. It was like listening to a choir of angels. When she had finished, she turned to me and said with a wink: "Now, if you practise hard, you'll be able to play that too." A few years of study passed and at last, as promised, I was able to struggle my way through the same piece. I couldn't (and still can't) play it very well, but nevertheless, I can't tell you how happy I was.

The point of that heart-warming insight into my childhood is this. I imagine that you've just spent a couple of hours of your life reading this handy volume. You've maybe tried a few of the ideas. But perhaps – and please forgive me for mind-reading again – you're wondering where to go next with all of this, and like me during those first few piano lessons, you're asking, is that it? Let me assure you, we set our own limits in life; we set our own goals and we really can achieve them – no matter what they are – if we want them enough.

The aim of this book has been to introduce ideas about how taking responsibility for ourselves, with the help of some useful and practical techniques, really can enrich our lives and make us happier people. The aim of this chapter is to see just how far we can take this. Now, don't worry,

In which we learn a thing or two from eight-year-olds

I don't expect you to do anything too dramatic, like running off to Australia to be a sheepherder – that's not what I'm suggesting. What I am going to do is to take a closer look at some of the assumptions that can limit us in terms of what we want to achieve and how we want to live, and see whether they are valid or not.

Now, typically, self-help books talk about the benefits of being stable and happy. While I wouldn't argue with the fact that "stable and happy" is a good thing, I think the benefits of going a bit crazy and being happy too are always undersold. Intrigued? (Please say yes . . .) OK, let me tell you a bit more about what I mean.

Happily crazy

What does crazy mean in this context? Well, what I mean by that is doing things that are often seen as being a bit risky in today's world. It seems that it is more important sometimes to drive the right car than it is to have fun, that it is more important to cling on to what we have than to take a risk. I want to suggest, gently, that going pleasantly crazy can be a real boost to our lives.

In which we learn a thing or two from eight-year-olds

We often have a great deal of expectations about ourselves – "I'm not the kind of person who . . ." – and there are often a great number of assumptions made about us that we accept without too much argument. These expectations can be, however, quite limiting. Let me give you a quick example.

My family went on holiday together once and it was an unmitigated disaster for reasons too ridiculous to go into here. As a consequence of this, I reached the ripe old age of 22 without ever having been abroad. One summer, I decided that enough was enough. My friends were all busy (well, the three friends I had at the time were all busy), so I had no other option but to go on my own. I booked a cheap flight to Ireland and a bed in a youth hostel then set off. I had butterflies in my stomach and was constantly asking myself if things that were happening were OK. Is the plane supposed to do that? Is it supposed to take half an hour for my bag to come off that conveyer belt thingy? I spent four days wandering around Dublin on my own, sightseeing, had a great time and then came back.

Now, when I got back from my trip and told people what I'd been doing, I expected comments

In which we learn a thing or two from eight year olds

such as "Cool! Did you have a good time?" Instead I got, "Why did you go on your own? How weird! I wouldn't want to go on holiday on my own . . .," and so on.

Now, it wasn't as if I'd decided to become a brain surgeon and spent five years working on the docks to pay for it, or anything particularly heroic. This is just an example of what, to me, was a little miracle and it also illustrates the way my actions were interpreted as a bit "crazy".

So, to sum up – what does "happily crazy" mean?

It means: deciding what you want to do, figuring out a way to do it and then doing it.

Nuts to expectations, to what other people think you should do, to what you think is beyond you and to accepting limitations. There is a whole world of experiences waiting for you if you want it. Hopefully, there has been enough in this book so far to suggest that our own thoughts, beliefs and the beliefs of others are just that – they are not cast iron facts that are beyond change. If we can change the way we feel about ourselves, if we can change the way we view the world, if we can start to feel happier and more productive about our lives, why stop there?

In which we learn a thing or two from eight-year-olds

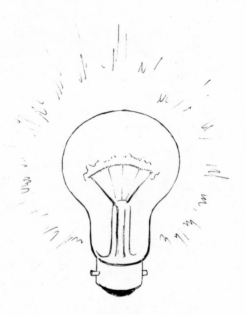

If you've always wanted to have green hair – why not do it? If you've always wanted to go to the cinema by yourself and eat popcorn until you're sick – why not do it? If you've always wanted to write love poetry, but were afraid of what people might think – why not do it? If you've always wanted to play the guitar – why not do it?

Limits

Now there are limits to what we can and cannot do, don't get me wrong – at 5ft 4ins, I'm never going to play professional basketball, for example. But, these restrictions aside, why must we allow the opinions of other people to set limits on what we do? And even physical and genetic limits aren't as important as they once were –think of the Special Olympics, look at the achievements of Stephen Hawking or even Beethoven.

I am not saying that unless you start coming up with revolutionary theories of physics while sitting on the toilet or writing sonatas in your coffee break that your life is somehow inadequate – not at all. What I am suggesting, however, is that you ask yourself why you should let your life be limited by what other people think you should do. What is the point of limiting yourself because of thoughts that have no basis in fact? Why not live a life that is, to you, extraordinary?

The implications of making small changes to the way we think are incredibly profound. Once we accept that we don't have to think that we are bad or stupid people, devoid of any talent, the

In which we learn a thing or two from eight-year-olds

sky can really be the limit. Once we start setting achievable goals for ourselves, the next step is simply to set another goal. Once we take responsibility for ourselves, success and failure cease to be an issue – there is simply living every day in a way that is closer to the way we want our lives to be.

Childishness as a compliment

If you were to ask 100 eight-year-olds what they dream of being, you would get a definite response from 99% of them – I want to be a train driver, I want to be a footballer, I want to be a princess or even, I want to be a train-driving, football playing, princess . . .

If you were to ask 100 33-year-olds what they dream of being, in a majority of cases you would be met with a blank stare.

Why? Where do all our dreams go? Why do we have to stop dreaming just because we have a mortgage?

Young children don't worry about whether they look silly to other people. They do what they can to maximise their happiness. They are quite Buddhist in this respect and we can learn

In which we learn a thing or two from eight-year-olds

a lot from their example. Why not allow yourself to be childish and silly from time to time? I don't mean by that, getting drunk at the office party and wearing a lampshade on your head. I mean allowing yourself to act in a child-like way – remember how uninhibited and enthusiastic children can be when they see something magical for the first time, like a rainbow? Since when was it a crime to have fun? Having fun keeps us young, keeps us interesting and expands our horizons. Ageing can be seen as merely a matter of how old we think we are. There is no age limit to setting goals – people learn new languages when they are 50, 60 or 70. Internet cafes are not solely the provinces of the young – new skills can be learnt all the time. Why not let that childish enthusiasm dictate what you do for a day or two? Use your imagination as a powerful tool to help you to change

Learning from children

On the day that I saw my first patient as a trainee psychologist, I was shaking with nerves. "I haven't got a clue what I'm doing," I confessed

In which we learn a thing or two from eight-year-olds

to my supervisor. "Not yet, you haven't" he said. "But remember, they don't know that. If you look confident, people will assume you are."

Think of the people that you admire. Why do you admire them? Is it because of their good looks and fame? Or is it because of something that they've achieved? Perhaps it's because of their outlook on life. Whatever the reason, why not adopt some of these characteristics – just for a day, an hour, a few minutes – and see how it feels? If it's confident people you admire – what does confident look like? How can you mimic it? If it's charming people you admire – why not be charming for a day?

Another characteristic that children have is the ability to play-act at the drop of a hat. One minute they're Spider Man, the next David Beckham. As adults, we frown on this, because it makes people unpredictable or "crazy". But what's wrong with a bit of unpredictability? What's wrong with greeting your girlfriend dressed like James Bond? (OK, enough of my personal life . . .) What's wrong with taking a step outside of yourself for a bit?

In which we learn a thing or two from eight-year-olds

Have an adventure

Children love to have adventures. Give them a couple of blankets and a pillow and before you know it, they've made a den. Give them a couple of pencils and a bit of paper and, hey presto, they've created a new world. Why not have an adventure? Who's to stop you?

Now this adventure doesn't have to be something mind boggling – to me, going to Dublin on my first overseas holiday was pretty spectacular. One patient of mine told me that the first time she'd gone to the shops on her own after years of being crippled with agoraphobia was "the most excitement I've had since I was little". The important thing is – what do you want to do? What's an adventure to you? Maybe it's cooking Chinese food for the first time. Maybe it's learning how to rollerblade. Maybe it's just going for a walk in the park and really listening and seeing what's going on around you. It doesn't really matter – what's important is that it's yours.

In which we learn a thing or two from eight-year-olds

Being cool

Let's Go a Bit Crazy

One of the advantages that adults have over children is on the whole issue of being cool. Now, I don't think I'm unique in the fact that I spent a large part of my teenage years trying to work out what was cool. For children it can be a real problem – if you're not "cool", you don't get invited to "cool" parties and you spend your Friday nights imagining that everybody else is having more fun than you are (wrong!).

Now, at an age when I'm too old to do anything about it, I can finally share with you the secret of being cool. Being cool is not about wearing a leather jacket and smoking cigarettes. Cool is not caring what people think. It's setting a target and reaching it, regardless of other people's expectations. It's not being limited by other people. Being cool is something that you can do today. Remember this fact – it's your life.

How do you want to live it?

CREATIVITY AND EXPERIMENTATION

As we have seen, children can be extremely creative and keen to experiment with all sorts of things, but as we grow up, many of us leave that enthusiasm behind. We let expectations about ourselves, and the influence of the opinions of others, stop us from doing things that are creative or a bit different. Creativity and experimentation are, however, very important life skills that can be useful in many different situations. It's not just about being able to paint a picture or play the guitar – it's about being able to think "outside of the box" in a different way; being able to come up with solutions to problems that seem insoluble; looking at a problem in a novel way; being able to use words metaphorically to illuminate a problem.

People often say "I'm not creative", in the same way that they often say "I'm not imaginative". I remember speaking to a patient who got quite angry at the thought that she might be creative or imaginative – then she revealed how she managed to juggle caring for three children, a part time job, all the cooking and cleaning in the house, and a myriad of other things as well. Now, to find solutions to these everyday problems really does take creativity! Experimentation can be seen as the practical application of creativity. Cooking is a classic example – the creative thought is "I wonder what this would taste like with a few more spices?" the experimentation is trying it. In the same way that thinking one positive thought can lead on to another one, so can a creative thought lead on to others. Think about what you do creatively. Is it the way you arrange the furniture to create an effect? The way you cook or dress? What do you do that's a bit different? Use it. Harness it. How can you be creative in your relationships, your friendships? How can being creative improve your work? The sky's the limit.

Chapter Ten

All Good Things . . .

*In which the author attempts to summarise and
ends up struggling with a metaphor*

Firstly, let me say, welcome to the end of this
book. I hope you have enjoyed it and that some
of the ideas contained herein have been useful
and interesting. Please feel free to contact me via
the publishers, if you have any comments, que-
ries or opinions (as long as they're polite). I hope
this book has been fun and I wish you all the very
best for your happiness and for the rest of your
life.

The world now offers us more opportunities than ever before – so many, in fact, that the
friendly alien who has been accompanying us on
our trip would be amazed at how much things
have changed in the last 100 years. Unfortunately,
the alien would also have spotted the conundrum

In which the author attempts to summarise and ends up struggling with a metaphor

that although we have more opportunities than ever before, the human race hasn't really become much happier.

Now, let me ask you a question – what is the biggest obstacle to feeling happy and changing the way our lives play out? Award yourself a gold star if your answer was "US!" and go to the head of the class. For everyone else, shame on you, please start again at the beginning . . .

Changing the record

Our lives can be seen like a record, metaphorically. It starts, plays certain songs and then, eventually, the needle lifts and the music stops. Luckily, if we don't like the music that is being played, we can change it. How do we do this? By altering the way we listen to the music, by changing the way the music is put together and by *dancing*. In the early part of the book, we looked at why people often feel bad about themselves, feel guilty or blame other people: they don't change the music. People follow the advice of the Negative Command Centre, which has accumulated all sorts of information that isn't

*In which the author attempts to summarise and ends up
struggling with a metaphor*

based on fact but which we pretend is. Imagine calling the Samaritans, only to find it staffed by people who don't like you!

So the first steps on the road to change are these:

- Know what you want to change.
- Dispense with problem-solving strategies that do not work.
- Take responsibility for your actions.

Now imagine this scenario. You have a friend whom you've known for years. Whenever you meet them, they speak aloud your worst fears about yourself. They tell you that the dress you are wearing doesn't really go with your shoes; that your hairstyle looks silly; that you shouldn't have spoken to somebody they way that you did; that you must behave in a certain way and that if you don't, you're inconsistent and strange. How long would you want them to be your friend before telling them in no uncertain manner to go and play with the traffic? But by criticising ourselves and putting limits on ourselves, we are doing exactly the same thing as the cruel friend.

In which the author attempts to summarise and ends up struggling with a metaphor

Listening to the music in a different way

The next steps can be likened to listening to the music of our lives in a different way. This is the strange thing about music – songs that some people love, others absolutely loath. I have seen people cringing in pain when I've played certain records (anyone remember the band My Bloody Valentine?) whilst the number one tune usually leaves me shaking my head and going "I don't get it". The point is this – we can hear things differently if we train our ear. How do we do this?

Look out for the miracles

Miracles don't have to be big. Start recognising small ones. Isn't it amazing that you can read these words? Isn't it amazing that you can feel the paper in your hands? Everyday miracles are all around us.

Start making positive connections

I used the metaphor of Happy Doughnuts or Sour Bagels. A Happy Doughnut is when we start to

In which the author attempts to summarise and ends up struggling with a metaphor

see happy or beautiful things, the chance of us seeing more of them increases. A Sour Bagel, on the other hand, is the opposite: if we think unhappy thoughts, the probability is that we will continue to think them and it will impact on our entire lives.

Describing the music in a different way

If we describe the music of our lives as boring, pointless, awful . . . well, it isn't going to be a popular soundtrack, is it? If we describe our lives as "full of possibility", there's no telling where it might end. The point is that if we change the way we use language to describe how our lives are going, we end up changing our actual lives. In other words, we learn how to Reframe and use the Language of Possibility.

If a musician plays the same notes over and over again – eventually, it gets a bit dull. If we Reframe, everything starts to sound different and we create more options. Just as important as this, we wrest back control of our lives – we start listening to the music we want to hear, instead of the music that someone else has chosen for us.

In which the author attempts to summarise and ends up struggling with a metaphor

Experiencing the music differently

Language is one of the most important things we have to help us describe the music of our lives. Language has permitted the human race to build the Great Wall of China, to construct the Basilica of San Pietro in Rome, to write the music of Mozart. We also have incredibly sophisticated equipment to play it on: our imaginations.

Our imaginations enable us to dream up different alternatives and options, and create the means necessary to bring these ideas into reality. In other words, we can visualise possibilities and because we are now using positive language and the language of possibility, there are no limits to what we can play.

Imagine this. Which album would you prefer to listen to: Life Is Grim by the Unfortunates, with songs such as Tough Times Ahead, It's Gonna Get Worse, How Will I Cope? and Misery – or, Dreaming by The Happy Weekends, which includes their hit songs Everything Is Possible, It All Starts Now, Happy To Be Me and Welcome To The World?

In which the author attempts to summarise and ends up struggling with a metaphor

Setting the hi-fi up

We can see our minds as the hi-fi on which we play the soundtrack to our lives (I'm not letting this metaphor go . . .). Sometimes, this needs a little adjusting to help us to hear the music better. At other times, however, when we want it to play us something soothing and fun, it plays something harsh and critical. The way to deal with this is to learn how to relax. This isn't as simple as it sounds, but it is a skill that we can learn. We can teach ourselves how to relax our minds, our bodies and our feelings, which make it easier to hear what we want to hear, when we want to hear it. We can also learn to ask our hi-fi for the right things. If we dislike boy bands, we assertively request that they are never played again, instead of aggressively shouting when they come on or passively accepting whichever songs are doled out to us.

Turn the volume UP!

Finally, we have looked at how all of this is just a beginning. From these simple techniques, we can really learn to listen to the music of the angels.

In which the author attempts to summarise and ends up struggling with a metaphor

There is no limit to what we can hear, no end to the choice of songs we can play and no reason to listen to the same old thing over and over again. Let me give you a heartfelt invitation:

Live the way you want to. Dream and bring your dreams into reality. Don't let anyone tell you you're not good enough and trust in yourself.

Appendix One

Useful addresses

The Citizen's Advice Bureau will also be able to help with information, contact them online www.citizensadvice.org.uk or look in your Yellow Pages for the nearest branch.

In England look at the www.nhs.co.uk website and search for "mental health services". In Wales look at www.direct.wales.nhs.uk and search for "emotional health". In Scotland look at www.wellscotland. info for information about mental health and access to services. In Northern Ireland see www.hcni. net, and nidirect.gov.uk.

There are also some fantastic charities that offer superb help and advice.

The Samaritans help people with innumerable problems every year and are just a phone call away.

Call them on 08457 90 90 90 or go online at <u>www.</u>
<u>samaritans.org</u> They now have an email service as
well and are responding to nearly 600 emails a day
at <u>jo@samaritans.org</u> You can reach them by post
by sending a letter to Chris at Freepost RSRB-KK-
BY-CYJK, P.O., Box 9090, Stirling, FK8 2SA.

MIND is a Mental Health Charity that can offer
advice and information about a wide range of
mental health difficulties. Their postal address is
Mind, 15–19 Broadway, London E15 4BQ, or call
/fax them on tel. 020 8519 2122, fax: 020 8522
1725. They have a good web site at <u>www.mind.</u>
<u>org.uk</u>. You can email them at <u>contact@mind.</u>
<u>org.uk</u> You can also phone the info line: 0300 123
3393. In Wales the number is 020 2039 5123.

Also check out The Scottish Association for Mental Health, wwwsamh.org, 0141 530 1000, and The
Northern Ireland Association for Mental Health,
www.niamhwellbeing.org, 028 9032 8474.

Another charity that does invaluable work in fur-
thering mental health advice is SANE. Call their
information line on 0845 767 8000. They have
branches in London, Bristol and Macclesfield and
a useful website at <u>www.sane.org.uk</u>.